# FIELD OF VISION

# FIELD OF VISION

## BY LISA KNOPP

UNIVERSITY OF IOWA PRESS

IOWA CITY

University of Iowa Press

Iowa City 52242

Copyright © 1996

by the University of Iowa Press

All rights reserved

Printed in the United States of America

Design by Karen Copp

Printed on acid-free paper

Library of Congress
Cataloging-in-Publication Data
Knopp, Lisa
    Field of vision / by Lisa Knopp.
        p.    cm.
    ISBN 0-87745-551-1 (pbk.)
        1. Visual perception.   2. Visual discrimination.   3. Perception.
    4. Human information processing.   I. Title.
    BF241.K62    1996
    814'.54—dc20                                    95-52045
                                                    CIP

01  00  99  98  97  96  P  5  4  3  2  1

FOR MY PARENTS,

JOSEPH KNOPP AND

PATRICIA PARRIS KNOPP

# CONTENTS

# ACKNOWLEDGMENTS

I gratefully acknowledge the contributions of those who read or talked me through parts of this manuscript: Hilda Raz, Fran Kaye, and Les Whipp at the University of Nebraska; my former office mate, Evelyn Funda, a keen and knowledgeable observer of the natural world who always put her own work aside to help me with mine; my mother, Patricia Knopp, who directed my vision to pheasants, mayflies, and other kin; my former husband, Colin Ramsay, who provided technical assistance and lessons in the art of seeing.

I would also like to acknowledge the editors of the following publications for the care they took with my essays: *Creative Nonfiction* ("Excavations," September 1995), *Farmer's Market* ("Sky Watch," Fall/Winter 1995, and "Edges," Fall/Winter 1993–94), *The Journal* ("Hard Remains," Spring 1996), *NEBRASKAland* ("Houseguest," August/September 1995, "Still Center," August 1993, and "Wildflowers," March 1992), *Cimarron Review* ("Seeing 'Possum," July 1992), *South Dakota Review* ("Field of Vision," Autumn 1990), and *Northwest Review* ("Pheasant Country," Summer 1990).

*But I saw these visions not in dreams, nor sleeping,*

*nor in frenzy, nor with the eyes of my body, neither did*

*I hear them with my exterior ears, nor in hidden places*

*did I perceive them, but watching them, and looking*

*carefully in an innocent mind, with the eyes and ears*

*of the interior man, in open places, did I perceive them*

*according to the Will of God.*

HILDEGARD OF BINGEN (1098–1179),
*The Visions of St. Hildegard*

# PREFACE

W hen we look directly at a subject, we move the eye so that the image falls on the fovea centralis, a tiny depression in the retina, smaller than the head of a pin. While our field of vision is spread over a 240-degree angle, we see only the 1.7 degrees covered by the fovea, because there vision is most acute.

Still, we can quickly discern quite a bit of detail. We do this by rapidly scanning, moving our eyes in quick, jerking, and largely unconscious movements so that one part of the scene after another falls on the fovea. To move from one image in the scene to the next takes only milliseconds. Within a few seconds we can construct a detailed picture.

This scanning process isn't as objective as it sounds. The eye does not indiscriminately pull details from the scene; the brain does not passively receive information from the retina. Rather the brain selects what it wants to see, ignores what it doesn't, and imposes expectations on what it does see. Since the eye is an extension of the brain, it obeys the brain's controls. Consequently, we are more likely to see what we believe is there than to see what actually is. If we are not alert and interested in the scene before us, we stop scanning, satisfied enough with a rough idea of the big picture that we do not bother with the details. How little of the world we actually see.

To see what is before us instead of what we imagine to be there means being present and alive in the here and now, a state of alertness that most of us seldom experience or can sustain for very long. And since most of the duties expected of us require single-mindedness, it is often counterproductive to be aware of the details of our surroundings. But the rewards for being able to experience this state of alertness at will are great. Consider the difference between two walks. On the first walk your gaze is inward: You replay conversations, explain yourself yet again to a real or imagined audience, plan the rest of the day, or the week, or the next few years. When you return home, you can barely recall the route you took. On the second walk, you keep your attention on the outer terrain—a herring sky, crows tearing pieces of road-killed squirrel, a child taking a wobbly first bicycle ride, gold and black caterpillars making lace of wild rose petals, a rock garden where each rock shows its best side. The first walk is a plate of cold leftovers; the second is a banquet table, heavy-laden with fresh, richly prepared foods.

But alertness isn't enough if we want to see the mundane as profoundly new. If what we perceive is a construct, as anthropologists, philosophers, and others tell us, then we need methods for suspending our judgments and expectations so the new may break through. I sought guidance from those who are more sighted than I—artists, naturalists, scientists, mystics. But most of all, I sought guidance from those who have committed themselves to a particular place, for they better than anyone else can see what dwells there. Without their guidance, I would not have known where pheasants nested in the summer or where to wait for beavers. Without their guidance, I might not have seen the pheasants and beavers when our paths crossed. Some of the experts I consulted suggested ways I could remove the motes from my eyes. Others left it up to me to discover methods for diminishing personal and cultural biases, for lessening my self-absorption, and for withholding or at least postponing my judgments. These essays document my journey toward vision.

I found my *mundus novus* in swatches and tufts of wildness in Iowa and Nebraska, the two places I call home. I had long been familiar with these two places, but through the discipline of seeing—of remaining alert and of making the eye innocent—I became intimate with them.

I feel an urgency to see and record the wild places I know before they are gone. Each day, I am reminded that the natural world is vanishing. A shopping center sprawls too close to Nebraska's only salt marsh. Songbird populations have declined by 30 percent since 1980 because of habitat loss. Unchecked agricultural runoff and industrial waste have placed the Mississippi, the Missouri, and the Platte on the list of endangered rivers at various times in recent years. If current legislation to gut the 1972 Clean Water Act is passed, most wetlands will be redefined out of existence. Experts tell us that the human population of the United States will double in the next sixty years unless we suddenly become dead serious about controlling our fertility. World population will double even sooner. In thirty or sixty years, will there be a place for shell-leaf penstemons and saw-whet owls? If so, how far will I have to travel to see them?

These essays were written between December 1989 and June 1995. I do not recall at what point I suspected that I could put the essays between two covers, a miscellany, bound by the voice of the first person singular and by their attention to the natural world. But I do recall that my friend and mentor Hilda Raz, poet, essayist, and editor of *Prairie Schooner*, first saw that each essay, either directly or indirectly, explored the act of seeing. I had written a book about vision.

The book charts a course. "Local Geography" examines the ways the physical terrain shapes the psyche of individual, community, and culture. "Pheasant Country" defines vision and the state of being ready to see. "Edges" details the limits or borders of vision; "Houseguest" considers the borders between inside and outside, wild and not wild, guest and host. "Excavations" explores the form I have chosen to contain my vision—the essay. "Sky Watch" is a meditation on the possibility of permanence; "Hard Remains" is a meditation upon the nature of memory and continuance. "Wildflowers" recounts my earliest awareness of a living essence; "Natural Resistance" explores the nature writer's or observer's responsibility to those essences. "Seeing 'Possum" explores the five-hundred-year history of what Europeans and Euro-Americans have and haven't seen when they have looked upon the opossum's tail; "Open Water" considers how a culture develops a symbol. Stalking a great blue heron in "Still Center" results in centeredness, a necessity for focused vision. Waiting for a beaver to emerge from her lodge further extends the examinations of boundaries in "Interiors." The attempt to identify an unknown bird "by the book" raises questions about the responsibility of remaining separate in order to name in "Field Guide"; learning to speak the language of nature is imagined in "Rustlings." Finally, the culmination of the process of seeing is presented in "Field of Vision," when merging with a cloud of mayflies heals the breach between subject and object, resulting in complete vision.

And that is what fully developed vision involves: the ability to erase the boundaries between self and other and become the object of one's perception, as did the child in Whitman's poem:

There was a child went forth every day,
And the first object he looked upon, that object he became,
And that object became part of him for the day or a certain part of the day,
Or for many years or stretching cycles of years.

I was never as present in the world as when I was in these essays. May the reader's experience be the same.

# FIELD OF VISION

# LOCAL GEOGRAPHY

~~~~~~~~~~~~~~~~~~~~~~~~~~~

> *Once in his life, a man ought to concentrate his mind upon*
> *the remembered earth, I believe. He ought to give himself up*
> *to a particular landscape in his experience, to look at it from*
> *as many angles as he can, to dwell upon it.*
>   N. SCOTT MOMADAY, Kiowa, "The Man Made of Words"

A disproportionate percentage of my essential knowledge came to me in third grade. I learned long division; mnemonic devices for spelling "arithmetic," "geography," "together," and "Mississippi"; that we were fighting Communism in Vietnam, and so it was a good fight (or so people said in 1965); and that one could choose not to believe in God. And it was in third grade that I saw my first map of Iowa. Not merely glancing, as I did when the Channel 6 meteorologist showed the temperatures for the Tri-State area (Iowa-Illinois-Missouri), but really seeing it, finding that it was not Burlington, my home-town, but Des Moines, the capital city, that occupied the center like a navel or omphalos around which life took shape.

We Burlingtonians were not solidly Iowan: we dwelt in the borderland. If Iowa's eastern boundary had been as straight as its northern and southern ones, we would have been part of western Illinois—"Forgottonia," as the denizens called it who saw their tax dollars spent on Chicago's problems. When I was eight, I knew only two things about Illinois: Abe Lincoln had lived there (I'd visited his house in Springfield), and the Illinoisans who came to Burlington to shop or be doctored didn't know how to negotiate short, steep streets and so my father was always honking and cursing at them. Our state's southern boundary was a straight line until Farmington, Iowa, where the boundary followed the Des Moines River to its confluence with the Mississippi just above Alexandria, Missouri. If the Des Moines had risen instead of dipped, we too would have a Confederate past.

It is human nature to see the space that we occupy as the center and everything beyond as decreasing in value the farther its position from our center. Ask people to draw a map of their home territory and they will exaggerate their own size and importance at their neighbor's expense. The people who had made the world map that hung in Mrs. Belaney's third grade classroom placed Europe, the North Atlantic, and the U.S. plumb in the center, split Asia, and shortened the entire Southern Hemisphere. But the Iowa map that hung in Mrs. Belaney's room had not been drawn by a Burlingtonian. My hometown was not the Europe but the Vietnam of our state.

Yet we were not as peripheral as the map indicated. The name of no other town in Iowa, perhaps the nation, was painted across so many boxcars. Our first famous railroad, the Burlington Route, had transformed the Central Plains. Charles Perkins, the second president of that railroad, lay buried in Aspen Grove, not far from my father's people. My father was a boilermaker for CB&Q, and even before third grade, I knew those letters stood for Chicago, Burlington, and Quincy, the great east-west route established in 1855. Since the CB&Q main shops were in West Burlington, I knew that my hometown was the most essential point on that line. When the CB&Q merged with the Great Northern and the Pacific Northern in 1970, the owners knew which city could not be dispensed with and named their line the Burlington Northern. My birthplace might not have been the capital of Iowa, but it was a railroading capital, and since railroads once ran the country, I figured it was as much a national capital as Washington, D.C.

The United States map further convinced me of Burlington's centrality. My river, the Mississippi, was 2,348 miles long, running nearly the entire length of the country. Though the Mississippi was not the spatial center of our continent, it was the functional center, the main artery, draining the vast area between Appalachia and the Rockies. Any river worth mentioning—the Rock, Iowa, Des Moines, Ohio, White, Arkansas, Red, and Yazoo—flowed into mine.

Even the wild Missouri, the only river that could hold a candle to my river, flowed into the Mother of Waters. Between Nauvoo, Illinois, and Montrose, Iowa (the latter, the place where my mother's mother's people had settled), the river was rumored to be its widest. Twenty-five miles north of this spot, Burlington was attached to the Mississippi like a gallnut to the trunk of an oak. We could not get any closer to the heart of the matter.

Henry Lewis, the early-nineteenth-century explorer of the Mississippi, said that Burlington was an amphitheater. The metaphor is as clear now as in Lewis's watercolor of the riverfront when Burlington was a town of 3,000, a little more than one-tenth its present size. The oval stage or arena is near the river, strung with railroad tracks and studded with typical riverfront edifices: a marina, a port, a train depot, a ship-shaped WPA auditorium, a post office, a courthouse, a few factories, and the grain elevators. Surrounding the arena are three sections: North Hill (churches and Victorian houses), West Hill (once the Swedish district where my father's mother was born and raised), and the comparatively newer South Hill. My metaphor: Burlington is a cupped palm.

Until I was twelve, I lived on Marietta, a three-block-long street about a mile west of the river. The 100 and 300 blocks were flat, but on different planes, since the 200 block where I lived was a precipitous hill cut into the more gently sloping West Hill. Marietta was too steep to climb in a good car when it snowed; it was too steep for the old junkers my father drove to climb in any weather; it was too steep for a child to bike down, since busy Division Street gaped at the bottom. Marietta was near the bottom of a valley, so we climbed a hill no matter which direction we went. But once we ascended West Hill, Burlington was open terrain, former tallgrass prairie where one saw far, found few places to hide, made few adjustments, and expected no surprises. The terrain changed little until one reached the east banks of the Missouri, 270 miles away.

Steep hills and rushing waters test one's faith. Before the Civil War, fishermen and towmen harbored their houseboats in the Willow Patch, then a largely submerged section of the North Bottoms. When my Federal Writers' Project guidebook to Iowa was written in 1938, the Willow Patch was dry ground where "simple and somewhat primitive" people wove fine nets and seines. During dry years, the Willow Patch is terra firma; during each of the major floods I remember—'65, '73, and the biblical flood of '93—it has become part of the Mississippi.

Even topography far above the river disappears unexpectedly. That same guidebook notes that the streets climbing the hills surrounding the business district do not run in straight lines for any distance. Rather, they angle off out of sight to avoid a bluff or to vanish over a hill. One must climb dozens of steps to reach some blufftop homes. Since Burlington's hills and valleys provide more spaces for people, trees, and buildings than a flat prairie mile, the closer one gets to the river, the more intense and concentrated the landscape becomes.

The cobblestone alley behind my Marietta Street house interrupted layers of crumbling sedimentary rock. Near the top of the alley, the stratified walls were low enough that small children could jump from them; at the bottom of the alley, the west wall was nearly twice as tall as my father. From my own reading, I learned that the fossilized trilobites, snails, corals, sponges, and other sea organisms that my brother and I tried to chip from the alley walls had accumulated on the floor of an ocean that had submerged North America more than 400 million years ago.

We were not the only ones drawn to these strata. A century earlier, Charles Wachsmuth, a German immigrant, began chiseling fossils when his doctor ordered him to spend time outside to improve his frail health. Frank Springer, a lawyer, settled in Burlington for the purpose of hunting crinoids after hearing Louis Agassiz lecture on them at the University of Iowa. The two men gathered the world's finest collection of fossilized *Crinoidea camerata* (star lilies attached by long stems to the sea bottom) from crumbling alley walls and riverfront bluffs. In a brick building at 111½ Marietta, the two men established the Wachsmuth Museum to house their collection. The collection is now in the Smithsonian Museum, and 111½ Marietta has been an unremarkable private residence for as long as I can remember. But the sea lilies remain unchanged in the walls where I once chipped their stems.

I believed the Devonian Sea belonged to the distant past until the summer of 1965, when the Mississippi rose to record heights. Films of volunteers building sandbag levees were televised on the national news, which I watched for the first time. My mother told me to write my Irish penpal, Groanne, about what I had seen of the flood, since she had probably heard about it on the news in her country. Despite my belief that my home was the center of the world, I was astonished to discover that people in other countries knew about the background against which I lived. So, I wrote her of impassable Highway 99 and of people evacuated to shelters because the twelve-foot stilts upon which their homes were perched weren't high enough to keep them dry.

The river not only gave shape to Main Street and the railroad tracks but exposed social stratification as well. Most of us wanted to live near the river, though only the richest and the poorest were able to. On the South Hill bluffs lived the obstetrician who assisted the births of my brothers and me; the Grandenettis, who owned nightclubs and were rumored to have Mafia ties; the

Leopold family, which had produced Aldo, the great ecologist and ethicist; Aldo's son, Luna, the expert on graded river systems; and Aldo's brother Frederick, who stayed home to guard wood duck nests and the family furniture factory. The middle class lived wherever there was not direct access to the river. Poorer river rats made do in trailers in the bottoms or in little houses near the levee, where they feared floods.

The river intends to put us all on equal footing, reducing the terrain through which it flows to a sea-level plain. Near its headwaters in central Minnesota, the Mississippi is "young," cutting deep, sharp V-shaped canyons, creating rapids, and gathering tributaries into itself. Between Rock Island, Illinois, and Cairo, Illinois, it is a "middle-aged" river, scooping broad, U-shaped valleys through which it flows more slowly, and midstream islands like our O'Connell, Baby, and Big. From Cairo southward, the Mississippi is an "old" river, meandering sluggishly through a valley so broad it is almost indiscernible. At some places, in fact, the water surface is higher than the land through which it flows. Once the river reaches the end of its course, it deposits its load of silt, which is why the Gulf of Mexico no longer bows as deeply into Louisiana and Mississippi as when the doomed La Salle searched for its mouth three centuries ago. A journey of 2,348 miles reveals what my stretch of the river once was, what it is, and what it will be.

People in bluffy Burlington "go down to look at the river"; people in flat Gulfport, Illinois (once East Burlington), "go up to look at the river." No matter which direction we come from, our readings of the surface are meant to keep the river in check, though nobody says as much. For those who don't make it down (or up) to the river, the *Hawk Eye* reports the previous day's levee changes and flood stages for a dozen cities from La Crosse, Wisconsin, to Keosauqua, Iowa. Thus when river people make small talk, we are not limited to the heat of the day or the height of the corn: "River's down another four-tenths. Never seen it this low."

My maternal grandfather often "went down to look at the river." When he lived in equally bluffy Keokuk, forty-two miles south of Burlington, this meant getting in his truck after supper, driving to the river, walking to the water's edge, and chatting with fishermen about the bait they were using. When he lived in a Burlington apartment halfway up South Hill, the river view from his front room window didn't scratch his itch. He and his dog, Duke, still went down to look at the river.

Though we couldn't keep the river in its place, it kept us in ours. While I often confused my right hand and my left, I always knew which direction I faced. The river was east even if I couldn't see it, and the universe was ordered in relation to that fact. The year and a half I lived near the La Moine River in Illinois, when I was in my late twenties, was the most disoriented period in my life because I could neither transfer my allegiances nor reorder my universe. Since I persisted in believing the Mississippi was east even when, in fact, it was west, I gave confusing directions and always felt slightly dizzy. The great river's presence then and now functions as my point of reference, my true east, my one constant. Without it, I am lost.

Shortly before I turned twelve, my family moved to a large house on South Hill, just three blocks east of a bluff from which I could view the river, the CB&Q bridge, McArthur Bridge, Big Island, and the floodplains of Illinois. Sometimes I biked to Crapo Park, where a wooden statue of Chief Black Hawk stood on the bluff, his hand shading his eyes. Squatters always came from the East, but once, Black Hawk had watched for them with the river behind him. After the Sauk and the Mesquakie were removed to Iowa, the river was always before him. When Iowa was opened to white settlers on June 1, 1833, Black Hawk retreated to a cabin first on Devil's Creek near Montrose and later on the Des Moines River, which he considered to be within walking distance of Burlington and the Mississippi. In 1838, six years before his people were removed to a bleak Kansas reservation, Black Hawk died. A blessing, I believe.

Everything I learned during the next several years moved me farther from the center. Geography taught that the Nile was longer, the Amazon wider, the Danube more picturesque, and other rivers—the Euphrates, the Yellow, the Indus—had watered powerful civilizations. I observed that boxcars came from places other than Burlington: Santa Fe, Rock Island, Milwaukee, Baltimore. And too, other places had prior claims on our name. In 1834 John Gray, one of our first white residents, renamed the Flint Hills (Shoquoquon, to the Iowa Indians) Burlington, after his Vermont hometown. Neither were the Burlington nylons, carpets, and winter coats advertised on television woven in textile mills in my hometown, as I had once believed; instead, they were produced in Gray's home state.

When I was thirteen, the Ament family moved in next door to my family, which was a boon for me, since they had three daughters close to my age. Though they had just moved from a different part of South Hill, Mrs. Ament made it clear that she was from The East, and by that she did not mean Illinois. Apparently, people in The East lived differently from the way we did. Mrs. Ament made leek soup (it looked like cream of onion to me), drank wine with dinner, "entertained" instead of "had people over." In her dining room hung a heavily framed family portrait that looked eerily artificial: all the Aments had removed their glasses; the photographer had somehow erased their blemishes and creases; they were bathed in soft light. Our family portraits were taken in harsh light in the parlor of Grace Methodist, and we looked like ourselves. Periodically, Mrs. Ament took her daughters Back East so they'd become familiar with Society. Apparently, Easterners were closer to the heart of society than we Midwesterners were.

Apparently, they thought differently than we did, too. An acquaintance of my mother's had been asked to write book reviews for a New York periodical on a regular basis. The magazine even offered to pay her. My mother's educated and sophisticated friend refused. "I'm too removed here in Iowa," she said. "My opinions are parochial."

It never occurred to me that geographical placement influenced how one read a book. I could imagine that *The Adventures of Huckleberry Finn* meant more to me than, say, to a Bostonian or a Seattleite. I'd seen the bed where Huck once slept in Hannibal, Missouri. I knew the way his bend of the river smelled and sounded. I, too, planned to leave civilization via the river. I would live in a cabin on a bluff overlooking the river, and I would never wear shoes, cut my hair, or go to school. My grandpa Parris, who would accompany me, would quit work, stop shaving, and hunt and fish all day. As much as I loved *Gone with the Wind*, I did not have the same geographical link with Scarlett and Melanie as I did with Huck.

But more than geographical familiarity kept my mother's friend from offering her judgments on books that people were writing and reading in other parts of the country. My mother's friend perceived a cultural gap between us and the readers of the New York periodical: not only were we at least a half year behind the coasts in the latest dances, fashions, and movies, but we *thought* differently than New Yorkers did. Before cable television and other world-shrinking technologies became ubiquitous, most influences, in my town and thousands like it, were local. Then, people were steeped in and affixed to the locality where they were born and thus were more disposed to being possessed by the landscape, in blood, bone, and brain. Such erratic terrain—here one day, gone the next—made conservatives of my townspeople. I do not mean in a political sense: when I was a child, blue-collar Des Moines County usually voted Democratic, though most Iowans were moderate Republicans. I mean conservative in that we are slow to change—jobs, hair styles, loyalties, diets—even if the change would better our lives. Stuck in river bottom mud, some might say. I believe a public library survey of patrons' reading tastes would reveal that the stories we most relish are about dull or stable environments where precipitous or mercurial characters do instead of are done to.

Gradually, I saw Burlington as the end of the world where nothing ever had happened or ever would. Certainly, what I learned in school reinforced, perhaps created, this attitude. American history seldom happened in my part of America; world history never happened in my part of the world. Since local history wasn't valued and thus wasn't taught (or vice versa), I learned little about where I was from and what it meant to be shaped by such a place. I started imagining ways to become something other than what I was. I studied Mrs. Ament, who was *in* Burlington but not *of* it. I studied television programs set in New York City or Los Angeles, from which I learned of commuter trains, muggings, and apartments reached by elevators. Sometimes when I was downtown, I kept my sights on the seventh story of Farmers and Merchants Bank and Trust, our tallest structure next to St. John's steeple. We, too, had a skyline. I tried to be on Roosevelt Avenue around five on a Friday afternoon (then, the only day banks were open past three and stores past five), because then and there traffic was so heavy that people sometimes had to wait for a second green light before they could go. We, too, lived in a hustling metropolis.

Much to my parents' dismay, during my midteens, I dreamed of converting to Judaism, the most exotic thing I could imagine for myself. The few Jewish people who lived in Burlington were all from other places: the family I baby-sat for were from Chicago; my classmate, Robin, whose Hanukkah party I'd attended, was from New York City; it was rumored that the parents of another of my classmates had survived Hitler's death camps. History had happened and was still happening to these people. Curiously, I could not see that for more than two millennia, the Jews' collective goal had been to end their exile and to re-root themselves in their place of origin. I could not see it was the deep story and not the topographical details that pulled me.

When I was in high school, my mother, brothers, and I traveled by Amtrak on my father's employee pass into Chicago on Saturday mornings and returned home in the evening. For us, Union Station, the bargain basement of Marshall Field, the lakefront, or the Art Institute were mere backdrop. Our sights were set on the Chicagoans, who with their wild clothes, fast pace, and impersonal demeanor were so unlike the folks back home. Though I was smitten with the Big City, I found it uninhabitable. It was dark and closed in, subway openings stank, taxi drivers drove dangerously, streets were dirty, the air was too "used." Since there were no hills to crest, there were no sudden surprises on the other side—an old acquaintance, a parade, an exploding grain elevator. Even the thin, cement-bottomed Chicago River was thoroughly predictable. Since it revealed only recently tossed trash or changes in the sky, nobody "went down" to check this river.

Isaiah predicted that his people would go into exile for "want of knowledge": because they had not made the stories they heard *mean deeply*, they did not understand the full implications of being a chosen people with a promised land. Neither did I understand that stories about home were stories about me. My lack of imagination banished me from my place of origin to a flat, river-less prairie city where I have employment (nothing secure), a marriage (nothing secure), and two children. If I had internalized the stories before my decision-making time, I would have been more ingenious and receptive; I would have found a way to stay where I belong. Like the Hebrew exiles in Babylon, I yearn for the day when my physical and spiritual centers will be re-aligned and I "shall never again be plucked up out of the land which I have [been] given" (Amos 9:15).

I know something of the last family who lived in my house in Nebraska based on the junk mail I still receive in their name, but I know nothing of their predecessors. A neighbor tells me that Guernseys chewed cud where my husband now mows grass. The buckling, faded barn a mile west of here where the cows were once milked is now surrounded by housing developments on three sides and a cemetery on the fourth. I read that the Oto and the Missouri hunted and farmed this knoll before they were forced to cede their lands in 1854. I read that this land, too, was once the floor of a wide and ancient sea.

And, too, I have personal history in this place of exile. When I was four, my father was transferred here to the railroad shops in Havelock, then just outside of Lincoln. What I remember most vividly from that period is not the half year of kindergarten I attended at Hartley School but how deeply my young parents missed hearth and kin. After a long, flat year and a half, they fled for the hills of Burlington. We stayed with relatives until our tenants' lease expired on our Marietta Street house, and my father welded farm machinery at J. I. Case Co. until CB&Q rehired him.

But my layers of personal history in Nebraska aren't as many, as deep, or as fossil-filled as those in Burlington. My family did not come to this Nebraska dairy to buy whole milk, though every time I see the faded barn, I remember jars of rich milk we bought from Anderson's dairy near Burlington. My parents eventually bought an acreage next to that dairy and lived there for a decade after I'd more or less left home. Twice I lived on that land—once while I was finishing college and later, with my small son, when I was commuting to graduate school in Forgottonia. On that land I learned the way the terrain unfolded five miles from the river, learned the rhythms of the dairy, learned the history of the surrounding farms.

In earlier times, a city or village center was marked by a sacred tree, a cathedral or temple, a central commons or market square with a fountain or statue.

Boundaries were often natural (a river, a mountain range, a forest) but included the human-made (walls, gates, fortifications, greenbelts). The purpose of boundaries was as much to keep a community's energy in as it was to keep outsiders out. Towns and cities were to grow within their boundaries, in a planned manner.

Once we observed this ancient and logical arrangement. For more than a century, downtown Burlington was the center where residents worked, worshiped, shopped, celebrated, socialized, banked, and were doctored, after which they returned to their outlying homes. Now if you walk Jefferson or Main Streets you will find one empty building after another, interrupted only by an occasional craft shop or restaurant, here today, gone tomorrow.

Burlington's population peaked at 33,000 during the Vietnam War, when the Iowa Army Ammunition Plant employed three shifts and frequently shook our foundations with underground bomb tests. But in the 1990s, my city of 29,000 sprawls amorphously westward, a new fast food, a new discount store each season as if it were a boomtown. In part, the reason for our loss of center is practical: if we don't observe the hundred-year floodplain, we won't get disaster relief money for the flood of '93 or following future floods. Only the rich or the foolish would establish a business near the river. But even more, this westward sprawl reflects a national trend in which the landscape has been reshaped to serve the motorist. The former sacred space of the town square, Main Street, or the central business district, where people once walked and talked, has been replaced by the "strip," a place seldom seen on foot or at slow speeds, a place where people interact only at drive-throughs or checkout lanes.

My family history is woven into the story of Burlington's expansion. In 1921 my paternal grandparents moved into a two-story frame house on a dirt road, still too country to be included in the 1938 map of Burlington. By the time I reached awareness in the sixties, my grandmother's stretch of Roosevelt Avenue (also Highway 61) was two paved lanes with our first pair of golden arches on one side, our first strip mall on the other. With the increased traffic, my grandmother began fretting over rumors that The State intended to widen Roosevelt Avenue in front of her house. In the mid-seventies, a sea of parking spaces and the enclosed Westland Mall pulled our center of gravity even further west, and my grandmother's home of fifty-some years was razed for the present Des Moines County Humane Society and a four-lane highway. She died within months of her forced removal. Dogs and cats are adopted or exterminated where I watered sweet peas and where my father cleaned the chicken coop. A wide-girthed elm in whose forked trunk I once sat shades the dog run.

Now, Burlington Medical Center is planning to leave the riverfront for a cornfield I sometimes biked past when I lived near the dairy. Hospital officials claim lack of parking has forced their move, but I believe they are responding to a lack of vitality: as more businesses and services move west, downtown is no longer a tangle of nerves and veins and ducts; rather, it is a bloodless husk. To move the hospital west is to exacerbate the problem, since hospital visitors and workers provide most of the downtown business, say city planners. To move the hospital west is to blur the boundary even more—parking lots and bean fields side by side. Even more, to lose the downtown hospital is to lose the site of our passages: there my two brothers and I were born, my grandmother died, my son was born, my great-aunt and grandfather died, and I passed a recent holiday with my father.

Since I mark my years away from home by the disintegration of the center and the boundaries in my hometown spaces, I am historical, a fact I have more easily escaped in other places I have lived. I am the second class to attend the new west-side high school—or not to attend the old high school at the end of Marietta Street. I worked at florists, taverns, and a hotel whose owners have since died, retired, or sold out. I took ballet lessons in a building that rented upper rooms to young Christian women who took their meals in the restaurant in the basement. After class, I walked a half block uphill to the library, checked out books, walked two blocks downhill to the Kresge dime store and caught the West Hill bus home. This month, the Kresge Building is a wig shop, last month it was a craft shop. The YWCA has moved to a new west-side building. Computer terminals glow beneath the marble busts of Burlington's founding fathers at Iowa's oldest public library (1896). A new, larger library building with better electrical wiring is in the works.

Because I am historical when I walk the hills of Burlington, there my sense of loss is most acute. But change is more easily integrated when witnessed. After the Great River Bridge opened to traffic in 1993, the old green McArthur Bridge that once sang beneath our tires was dismantled, floated downriver piece by piece, and sold as scrap metal, an ignoble end for such a noble bridge. My children, husband, parents, and I watched a middle section float down and lodge against ice from a window in Burlington Medical Center, where my father was hospitalized the Christmas of 1993. To have found the bridge of my childhood gone without a trace, as I did the old Corse school building or my grandmother's house on Roosevelt Avenue, would have been deeply unsettling. But I witnessed its passing, bid my farewells, and so the record is complete.

One thing that has not changed in my lifetime is the churches of downtown Burlington. These are not the modern warehouse churches that spring up at the edge of town like thistles but solid stone structures cut into hills, nestled between two buildings, the sacred and the profane side by side. Zion Church, where my father was confirmed, abuts the phone company on the north, a Masonic lodge on the south. This church is a descendent of Old Zion, where the legislature met when Burlington was the first territorial and state capital. The gothic First Methodist, which my great-grandfather Frieberg, a Swedish stonemason, built of jasper in 1889, rubs elbows with the empty building that once housed Osco Drug (since moved to the mall) and Prugh's funeral home, where my father's people are laid out when they die. The spireless Grace Methodist, where I was confirmed, was solid enough to survive a fire.

The grandest church of all is St. John's Catholic, whose interior I've yet to see. The hill it rises above is magnificent: "Half a mile west of the shore at this point the view is unusually grand and romantic, extending over dense forests and wide prairies," wrote Henry Lewis. The dense forests are gone, but the view remains: from this hill I can see most of downtown, the river, and deep into Illinois. When I returned from my trips to Chicago, the church built upon this hill was my first assurance that I was home again.

The steeple that extends the hill is my sacred tree, the great vertical marking the center of the world, a ladder where angels descend and ascend, like the spot where John the Revelator saw "that great city, the holy Jerusalem, descending out of heaven from God." To earn my photography badge in Girl Scouts, I photographed the valley, the hill, and my *axis mundi* at different times of the day in different weather from my second-story bathroom window on Marietta Street. But I was disappointed: the small black-and-white pictures were so cluttered with rooftops, treetops, and electrical lines, I could not see where the slim steeple pierced the heavens.

"All of us carry within us a picture of that terrain that was learned roughly between the ages of six and nine," says poet Gary Snyder. Like baby ducks, we are imprinted with the image of our geographical mother. To live away from the home territory whose likeness we carry within is to be out of place: it is to live in exile. Yet one does not have to leave home to be away from home. Snyder suspects that tens of millions of North Americans, though physically born in a place, do not actually live there intellectually, imaginatively, or morally.

Neither must one physically inhabit a place to be at home there. One's roots may be plunged so deeply in a specific place that she can never leave that place, no matter how far she travels. The Black Hills are home and sacred ground for the Lakota even when they live in distant cities. Israel is home for many Jews who have never set eyes on it. Though I live on the prairie, I write of the river. In my dreams I walk the bluffs and bottoms. I collect story upon story about the forces that created the physical and cultural face of home and weave those into my memories of home. I make frequent pilgrimages to the center. Like other exiles, my continuity and rootedness comes not from the reality of an entire life spent at the same bend of the river, working, worshiping, grieving, celebrating with other people shaped by the same terrain, but from the memory and the promise of such a place.

Barry Lopez, who writes often of what it means to be intimate with a place, says that "the shape of the individual mind is as affected by land as it is by genes." The inner landscape of those who call my place of exile their home is flat, wide, and windburned. Except for those days when it's winter in the morning and summer in the evening, the days have a level sameness about them and the people reflect this unwound, flatland predictability. But my inner landscape rises and falls sharply near the center, relaxes and unfolds toward the edges. My lot is to tend to the wide middle, where fast waters dislodge and drag my depths and cut my rocky bluffs. My moods are deep and many: I am cold but open waters where eagles roost and dive; I am warm, still slough waters where lily pads drift; I am gray and rushing waters that moisten fields one year, that swallow them the next. My heart and mind are shaped in the image of home and center. A hundred dry, flat prairie years cannot erode this erratic, watery, fossil-filled, story-filled terrain.

Spring 1994

# PHEASANT COUNTRY

*I*t was a mild, snowless December morning. The road, the fields, the barren trees, even the sky were shades of dun and gray. I was half listening to the news on my car radio—something about the U.S. invasion of Panama and the near-fatal shooting of the local deputy sheriff—when suddenly, to my left, in the fringe of brush and saplings that parted two cornfields, I glimpsed a flash of burnished rust and iridescent blue and the sweep of a long, extravagant tail. The image held just long enough for me to recognize what I had seen, though not long enough for me to scrutinize the parts before it dissolved into background. Pheasant. A detail that startles with the suddenness of memory or insight, unexpected and fleeting.

They are not native to this region. Their places of origin are east: China, India, Asia Minor. But much has happened since that time of origins.

Fact and myth merge to reveal the genesis of the *Phasianus colchicus*. Legend has it that when the Argonauts, those Greek heroes consumed with more timely matters than the pros and cons of introduced species, departed from ancient Colchis on the eastern shore of the Black Sea, they departed with more than just the Golden Fleece. Aboard the *Argo*, they freighted homeward the exotic black-necked birds so abundant at the mouth of the Caucasian river, the Phasis. From Greece the birds were carried to Rome. According to H. B. C. Pollard in his 1929 *Game Birds*, evidence "mainly gastronomic in trend" associates the arrival of the black-neck pheasant in England with the arrival of the earliest Romans.

Since those legendary times, the pheasant has continued to be a hardy and desirable settler. Moreover, he is one of our earliest European immigrants. In 1790, Ben Franklin's son-in-law, Richard Bache, released the first shipment of English black-necks in the wilds of New Jersey. They dispersed, as did those in subsequent releases, establishing themselves throughout the East and Midwest.

Then about a century later, O. N. Denny, the American consul general in Shanghai, trapped a hundred pairs of Chinese pheasants, each possessing the full white circle about the throat—hence the name "ring-neck"—and released them in Oregon's Willamette Valley, where they prospered beyond anyone's expectations. Only seven years later, in 1893, there were, as Gene Simpson states in the 1814 *Oregon Fish and Game Commission Bulletin*, "more Chinese pheasants in Oregon than in the whole Chinese Empire." Others followed Denny's example, transplanting Old World stock to the American wilderness. Fewer than five hundred birds were introduced into the northern prairies before 1905, but this easily assimilated alien grew like ragweed in an abandoned field, thriving everywhere north of the Mason-Dixon Line in the continental states, so that by the 1950s he was considered a pest in some regions and farmers opened their lands to unrestricted hunting. Though their numbers have plunged in recent decades because of habitat loss and the popularity of those farming practices that eradicate all but the single planted crop, pheasants are still plentiful enough to be declared legal game in thirty-four states.

Yet, despite this reputed abundance and despite the fact that the two places I call home—Iowa and Nebraska—are in the very heart of pheasant country, I have seen only that one bright flash this season.

Pheasants are elusive creatures. Every hunter knows this. Those orange-vested sportsmen who pull their pickups onto the shoulder of my road willingly share their stories. They tell me that as long as they remain in the truck, a pheasant will offer himself, but once they step out of the truck and raise their guns or field glasses, their prey vanishes into the scantiest cover. Sometimes, into thin air. And even if the birds linger, they possess the unnerving ability to flush just beyond shooting range. What is more, some hunters claim that the cannier cock birds know exactly when the season begins and ends and they disappear for the duration. The real wonder, then, is not that the pheasant can make himself so scarce but that anyone has ever seen one, much less bagged one. For a long time, in fact, European naturalists believed that these fantastic, ephemeral creatures were mere figments of the imagination of Chinese artists, thus dismissing the birds and the claims of their creators. After all, who can believe what she cannot see?

I could say that I haven't yet the eye for pheasants. They must be before me, feeding in the white and tan of snow and corn stubble, but I do not see them. And this inability to see what is before me is not unprecedented. Some people find enough morel mushrooms each spring to fill a skillet several times over, while I have never found a one. Two of my friends harvest hundreds of dollars' worth of wild ginseng each year, not in China or Korea but here, in eastern Iowa, though the herb vanishes before my eyes. And arrowheads. To some eyes—those of Tony Bakutis, a retired meat cutter from Springfield, Illinois, for instance—this area is positively littered with the flint projectiles, some of the preciser ones no larger than my thumbnail. Bakutis, who has one of the finest collections in the Midwest, says that this area was once the political and cultural center of a prehistoric Indian confederation. Hence, the ground beneath our feet is rife with the flints. Or at least it is to Bakutis's eyes. Several thousand artifacts are stacked in cigar boxes, floor to ceiling, in his basement, den, and closets. And how did he come to see all these? Happenstance. Twenty-five years ago, as he walked a newly plowed field, the farmer accompanying him bent to pick up an arrowhead uncovered by the plow and handed it to Bakutis. Since then, Tony's vision has been honed in on arrowheads.

Bakutis is a man who knows about seeing. He knows the initial difficulty of distinguishing the thing to be seen from its cover: "The country is full of lost arrowheads—lost arrowheads that will never be found. In timber, where they don't cultivate, they'll never find them." And he knows the possession that can result once the eye becomes informed of and receptive to an object. In fact, he delivers a warning. Someday, while innocently walking along, we might see a flint, pick it up, and "zap," we shall be hooked. "So you see finer material. So you start wanting it! So you start looking more. And then . . . the bug can really bite you."

In truth, even if I did see these hidden things for myself, there would be no certainty or finality about the experience, since the process of seeing and identifying continues even after the image is gone. And, too, the process must begin before the image appears, since it is but the rarest individual who can distinguish the thing from the background, the pheasant from his cover, without prior knowledge of the thing to be seen. In other words, I must be ready to see pheasants. I had seen illustrations of the bird in flight on the covers of *Field and Stream* and like periodicals on the grocery store magazine rack. And, on more than one occasion while bumping over midwestern backroads, someone has called out, "Pheasant!" and I have glanced, perhaps disinterestedly, I confess, yet long enough for a link to form between the shape and the name. Consequently, on the mild December morning when the United States invaded Panama and the local deputy sheriff was gunned down while trying to make an arrest, I knew that I had seen a pheasant. And arguably, without this preparation I would not have seen it at all. Still, I demanded verification.

Verification was easily obtained. When the previous owners of my brother's Mississippi River cabin made their final migration to their Florida retirement home, they left behind a seedy collection of stuffed and mounted game birds, one of which, a bedraggled pheasant, pauses in midstep on the table next to my IBM Selectric even now as I write. If it were not for this frozen bird, I would know little of the actual size or shape or coloration of the *Phasianus colchicus*. The bird I witnessed in the field was too far, too fleeting, the day too overcast, my eye too uninformed for me to impose anything more definite than "a flash of burnished rust and iridescent blue and the sweep of a long, extravagant tail" upon the image. But now I can infer not only that the bird I witnessed possessed coppery breast feathers but that the edges of those feathers were lined with black. His neck was not simply blue but blue-green, abutted by nearly flattened white crescents, one on either side. In the front and back, darkness. My field guide to North American birds pictures the full white neck ring that earned the bird his common name, but honestly, this distinguishing mark does not exist to my eye. Likewise, my field guide pictures a hexagonally shaped red patch with a black brow of sorts beneath the actual eye. But these markings no longer—perhaps never did—exist on my mounted rooster. About the eye, he is worn to the brittle skin, only short black tufts of feathers remaining. I will not believe in red eye patches or solid-white collars until I see them for myself.

This late autumn, I walk country roads with an eye for pheasants. I know their haunts: weed-choked fencerows, stream-bank thickets, grassy ditches, fields gone to pasture, cattail sloughs, the inclines along abandoned railroad tracks. And I know their time of day: they are day-active, especially, according to one veteran pheasant watcher, at dawn and at dusk when they appear on the gravel road to eat grit. I reasoned that I had only to position myself in those places at those times and the rest was simple: indeed, the rest was up to the pheasant.

So I walked, scanning the miles of flat fields broken only by silos, clusters of farm buildings, bladeless windmills, a hill full of twisted apple trees, and a blinking radio tower. I pulled my gaze in close, scrutinizing flat fields broken by borders of barbed wire, foxtail, and dried milkweed stalks. But I saw not a single pheasant. Clearly, these birds know when they are being stalked. Whether this ability is motivated by caginess or shyness, whether it is instinctive or learned, I do not know, but it did demand a reckoning. Consequently, I changed my strategy. If they knew I had been pursuing them, I would stop. I would simply walk. I would walk to the highway and back to exercise my dog, Elsa. For diversion, I would walk the neighbor's private lane that wound through shallow bowls of timber. I would walk the mile to the Tradin' Post for some essential commodity—a box of dog biscuits, a jar of pickle relish. If I felt compelled to scan the trees for birds, I would watch for red-tailed hawks, equally regal though less discreet.

With my change of strategy, the pheasants began to appear, though sparingly, unexpectedly. The first one came to me when Chandler, the neighbor's black Lab, flushed a rooster from the snow-covered underbrush in a stand of timber. The bird flew from the ground to a high cedar branch, his back toward me. I needed no field guides or stuffed birds to tell me what I had seen. It was all there, apparent to the eye: the blue-green neck, the red eye patch, the orange breast feathers scalloped in black, the broken flash of white about the neck. More there than I had the time or ability to receive.

He turned his head and gazed at me one moment before lifting and sailing across the adjacent cornfield. Finally, in the distance, he was nothing more than a dragonfly with his narrow body and parted tail. Here and gone. Catch it if you can.

If my only sense had been in my eyes I would have missed him, even if I had been looking. Yet, at that instant when the dog flushed the bird, I was stunned into awareness. This pheasant wanted to be heeded. He was demanding my attention with what I could not ignore: a great rush of wild wings and a startled, piercing cry.

I have heard it before, that great explosion of wings. It is the sound that precedes emergence—whether of wild geese on the pond or of seemingly lost dream images—of anything from its natural cover. But that cry lies on the outer reaches of recognition. It does not seem to be of the world I inhabit. Nor can I describe it. It is not enough to compare it to the soundless shriek of disclosure uttered by the white grubs and beetles that skittered to retain some just lost state when I overturned a small boulder in my backyard. It is not enough to compare it to the cry of terror I exchanged with an amber-eyed doe when I turned my car headlights onto a dark country road.

Other people have tried to describe this cry. They say it is a cackle, a crow, a squawk. Even though they speak of its startling eeriness, I cannot believe they heard the same sound I did. I can only say that this is the very sound of wildness at the moment it is being lost forever.

I am told that pheasants use the hayfield across the road as their breeding grounds. There, they camouflage their ground nests with grass, lay their clutches of half a dozen or so olive-green eggs, and raise their chicks, teaching them to scratch for seeds and bugs, perhaps teaching them to drum their wings and cry. While all of this is going on, the adult pheasants openly enter and exit the field. I suppose that there is even a courtship ritual worth watching that precedes all this, but I have never witnessed it and probably won't. At least not in that field in the near future. The man who farms that land, the same one with whom my friend Chandler resides, plowed the field this fall, leaving slim pickings for the bird population. Moreover, he intends to plant his field in corn this spring, one crop only, no weeds, fence to fence. Not enough cover or privacy or edibles for a young couple and their brood. This will send them packing.

I could have observed the pheasants last spring and summer, but then my world was crowded with what I expected and yearned for in the spring: larks and finches, blossoming apple trees, wild carrot, new-green cornstalks and the return of the raccoons that nest in the hollow tree this side of the pheasant field. Against all this, I admit, the pheasant loses his luster.

Could this rush and cry really be taught or is it simply uttered, prompted by something undeniable . . . in the genes, in the marrow, or in some place less easily found or named? It is a rigged question. I already know the answer, and it is an answer grounded not in what I've observed in the pheasant field or learned from pheasant hunters or read in any brittle-paged monograph on the *Phasianus colchicus* but rather in what I've observed about the occasion of the rush and cry among members of another species: *Homo sapiens*. These sounds alert me to an approaching blaze of brightness, sudden as a spasm of lightning on a summer night, among those who people my world. These sounds—whether of their making or of my own, I cannot say—direct my attention so I may see the bright release among their words.

The rush and cry was there, for instance, when I heard a Mount Pleasant, Iowa, violin maker admit that he must first become acquainted with a raw piece of wood and learn of its willingness before he can ever begin crafting the instrument. It was there when I heard the champion horse cutter from Geneva, Nebraska, disclose that the secret to his record time was in singling out a cow "that has a lot of look to it" and then pursuing it. It was there when the resident of the nursing home where I once worked as a cook assured me, as she gazed from the dining room window onto the municipal swimming pool below, that through the darkness she could detect the lights from her menfolks' lanterns as they returned from the river. And finally, I heard the rush and cry as I read the journals of the Fort Madison, Iowa, physician Albert C. Richmond, who claimed that when he applied poultices of old bread and milk to open wounds, they healed faster than when he applied only fresh bread and milk. Trusting what he observed, he began buying day-old bread from local bakeries for half a penny a loaf and storing it in a dampened condition in the cellar or haymow. Then he instructed his sons to fill capsules with a white powder—aspirin— and a damp, gray, odorous substance—mold. Note the following excerpts from Dr. Richmond's notebooks:

September 9, 1900. Robert S., age 18. Acute tonsillitis. Temperature 104. A very septic throat. I tried to give mouldy bread, but parents refused to give it.

September 10, 1900. Robert is still very ill. Giving mould with asprin in capsules. 3 capsules, 4 times daily.

September 11, 1900. Robert's improvement is unbelievable—more rapid than typhoid or enteritis. I shall give all patients with fever and infections, mould. If I should tell the other doctors about this, they would think I am crazy.

Avoiding the judgment of patients and colleagues alike, Dr. Richmond secretly administered penicillin twenty-nine years before Sir Alexander Fleming's official discovery of the drug and forty-five years before this discovery was acknowledged with a Nobel Prize.

When I hear the words of these people and others like them, I hear the beating of wings, alerting me that something wilder and deeper than reason is being tapped. And really, it is not that wildness is being forever lost, but rather that it is being exchanged: a parcel of wildness for a moment of vision, that unearthly cry marking the precise moment of the alchemical conversion. I cannot speak of the mechanics of this exchange because it lies within the realm of the miraculous. But I have witnessed the release of something raw and vital that precedes this exchange, and I have witnessed the resulting vision. It is a vision that guides one to see delicate flint projectiles on woodland floors. It is a vision that allows one to penetrate the being of another, whether a block of wood or a frightened calf. It is the vision that allows one to exist completely in whatever time and place is before her, whether real or imagined, past or passing or to come. It is the vision that not only offers hunches or insights but provides the faith and will to follow them. Indeed, it is the vision that comes to those in pheasant country.

Pheasants are not native to this region. Thus, pheasant country is a place to be not found but made. If we hope to fill our winter fields with bright flashes of rust and blue, we must invite them in the spring, though our world already seems full. We must plant our fields diversely, abundantly, and not tend them so carefully that no wilderness remains along the edges. When we harvest, we must not be so thorough that nothing remains for our wild ones to feed upon when the days are thin and cold. When we look, we must look with eyes that are sensitive and discriminating. We must receive not only what is directly before us but what flashes along the periphery as well. If reason or learning or expectations blind us, we must allow the pheasant to direct our vision with whatever means he possesses. And then we will find ourselves living in the heart of pheasant country, bestowed with the gift of vision that the pheasant brings.

December 1989

# EDGES

~~~~~~~

*It is a matter of transitions, you see; the changing, the
becoming must be cared for closely.*
LESLIE MARMON SILKO, Laguna, *Ceremony*

The north side of the prairie is burning, yet is not being consumed. As I
draw closer, I see forked flames transform themselves into a ribbon of
green and pink-red leaflets and firm torches of burgundy berries.

Toward the center of the grove, the open, flat crowns are heads and shoulders above me, but nearer the edges we see eye to eye. Some of the outliers are
only knee- or waist-high. This plant defies classification. Because its angular
stalks are woody and gnarled, it cannot be grouped with the supple, green-
stemmed goldenrod, blazing star, and purple coneflower. Because its stalks are
single instead of many like the hazel, chokecherry, and wild plum, it is not a
bush. With its compound leaves—about twenty leaflets per frond and a count-
able number of fronds per stalk—it is too sparsely leafed to be grouped with

the cottonwoods, elms, ashes, and hickories, which may produce as many as one million leaves per growing season in their maturity.

I cannot say if the sumac's fiery life is one thing or another.

Sumac is a border plant, flourishing in those transitional areas where two vegetational types meet. Upland to lowland, for instance. In 1804, Lewis and Clark reported that sumac colonies were quite common on the steep declivities of the Black Hills where the Cheyenne River meets the Missouri, because there they were "sheltered from the ravages of fire." But the report says nothing of sumacs either on the crest or in the valley.

Sumac also abounds in the margin between woodlands and grasslands, whether that be the clamorous forest fringe between prairie stream and upland or the wider "tension zone" between eastern deciduous forest and tallgrass prairie.

John E. Weaver, University of Nebraska plant ecologist and prairie conservationist, conducted a number of studies in Nebraska and Minnesota sumac thickets to discover what made this transitional zone possible. Sumacs propagate through rhizomes, some of which Weaver traced more than twenty feet from the thicket edge, their course marked by the presence of erect roots. He learned that these sumac "pioneers" make soil conditions more hospitable by increasing the water content of both the air and the soil, modifying the texture and composition of the latter. Because the shrubs serve as windbreaks and their shade reduces both light and temperature, humidity is increased and the evaporation rate decreased. Because of the rich mulch of fallen leaves and the blown plant debris lodged among the sumac trunks, runoff from rain or melting snow is sharply reduced. To prove the higher moisture levels, Weaver placed atmometers within the thicket and twenty-four meters away in open prairie. The first ten inches of soil beneath the sumac thicket was 6 percent moister than soil of the same depth beneath the grasses. Moreover, the soil remained moister to a depth of five feet. After Weaver measured the growth of bur oak seedlings planted in prairie, scrub, and forest zones, he reached the not-so-surprising conclusion that the tension zones where sumac thrives are wetter, cooler, darker, and stiller than the grasslands, yet drier, warmer, brighter, and windier than the woodlands. Neither prairie nor woodland, but a little bit of both.

The leaves of those sumacs on the dry, sunny bank tops pink early in September; those near the shady forest's edge wait until the calendar turns. But when the leaflets of the sumacs on the hillsides are equally red and green, I know the day belongs not to summer, nor to autumn, but to the fine line between the two seasons. By the time the sumac is mostly pink and red, the elms and cottonwoods have yellowed and thinned. When the sumac leaves are dark like red plums and their leaflets droop back from the petiole, I know I am far from the edge: it is the heart of autumn.

Prairie sod is tough and dense; prairie summers are hot and dry. Without the sumac thicket, the forest could make little progress in its invasion and conquest of the hostile grasslands.

Botanist Henry A. Gleason says that soil conditions created by the sumac permitted the forest to conquer the grasslands in two different ways. First, the forest followed the sumac up the lee side of rivers and streams, where moisture was still relatively certain. There, trees with winged seeds—cottonwoods, green ashes, elms, silver maples—gained a toehold. Close at their heels came those plants bearing edible fruits, such as hackberry and wild cherry. Closing up the ranks were the slower-moving oaks, buckeyes, hickories, and Kentucky coffee trees.

Through a second line of attack, the forest followed the sumac onto the uplands perpendicular to the streams. The shade from the sumacs and other shrubs such as hazel and wild plum, as well as the shade from the forest canopy, so weakened the prairie sod that tree seedlings were able to put down roots. As the sumacs and other shrubs led the forest onto the prairie, those shrubs bringing up the rear died. They were replaced by trees while at the same time a new outer edge of pioneers shot up on the prairie edge of the thicket.

Again, a predictable procession followed the advancing sumac tide: new seedlings came in advance of the parent trees; then, the herbaceous, shade-loving plants; finally, those herbs that needed humus. While the shrubs advanced onto the prairie at a pace of about thirteen feet per year, Gleason says that places exist along streams "where trees are growing more than a mile beyond their extreme limit of only fifty years ago." In other words, the forest moved about a hundred feet per year. If agriculture and human settlements hadn't halted the forest's westward advance, the wood might have moved toward Dunsinane even faster. A real cutting edge.

In the simplest sense, an edge is that part farthest from the heart or center. It is the line where one thing ends and another begins—day and night, silhouette and background, faith and doubt—so the edge is simultaneously the outermost limit of two different things.

Philosopher Avrum Stroll says that nothing can be an edge "without some degree of linear extension in one direction, and thinness in another," though how much of either is hard to determine. Widen the edge and it becomes a surface. Shorten its linear extension and it is but a point. Like surfaces, edges are not identical with the object possessing them: they are merely a slender portion of the whole. Thus edges are slippery, relative affairs that can be characterized only in relation to the entire object. We cannot speak of the sumac edge, then, without speaking of the forest and the prairie.

But is the edge real or is it an abstraction? Stroll answers, both. An ivory cube has six sides, each of which is a face of the cube. Just as there is no hiatus between the two hemispheres of the globe—nothing, say, that is not north or south—neither is there any place on the die that is not part of one side or the other: the sides are in direct contact with each other, and the entire surface of the cube is consumed in the six sides. So where, then, asks Stroll, are the twelve edges of the die? If edges belong to the outermost part of the cube and are real, they occupy space, which means that the six sides are not in contact with each other. Yet the eyes and the fingers sense otherwise. "The compelling conclusion to draw from this line of reasoning," says Stroll, "is that the edges that 'separate' the surfaces are not substantial, i.e., are not embodied. Instead they are abstractions, functioning in much the same way that the equator does when it separates the two hemispheres." This line of reasoning leads to the curious conclusion that an edge is an interface with no divisible bulk, yet is able to separate contiguous media from one another.

But edges are more substantial than that, Stroll says. The edge of an ivory cube can be smooth or jagged; we can balance the cube on its edge; we can paint the edge red. None of this is possible if the edge is immaterial. In truth, an edge of the cube is the outermost part of the surface or face. The edge is a physical entity. No mere abstraction. Real.

The mind and the eye tell different stories about an edge. Because an edge is the line where two things meet—white moon and blue sky, water and land, my curved palm and my baby's head—I judge it to be a shared thing. Yet, to speak of the edge of the water, the moon, my hand, reflects not what I know but rather what I see: that edges belong more to one than to the other. Sketch a sumac leaf and you will see what I mean.

It would appear that I assign the edge to that which has the sharper form or larger mass. Any visible celestial body—even a paper moon—has mass and form, while sky does not. Though land has more substance than water (I can't, say, walk on the latter), I still speak of the water's edge, though I cannot explain why. In the case of my child and me, we both have form and substance, though the amount of the latter differs between us by about a hundred pounds; so, the edge between us is mine. If ownership of the edge were determined by what I know best, I would attach it to the sky (I've never been to the moon, but I'm breathing sky every moment); the land (other than a few Mississippi River excursions, I've lived a landlocked existence); my hand (thirty-some years older than my baby's sweet curls). Yet the world is not as consistent as any of this.

If I shut one eye, the world becomes one-dimensional. The moon is hung on the flat surface of the sky. Water rests on the earth's unbending surface. My hand cups my baby's head. I believe my eye when it is single: the edge belongs to that which is outermost.

If this theory is correct, then the sumac edge belongs to the prairie. As botanist Peter Bernhardt tells the story, less than 11,400 years ago, a mere shudder in vegetational history, the aboriginal spruce and pine forests had already been replaced by oak woodlands, which, in turn, fell to the advance of the true grasslands. It took Konza Prairie in the Flint Hills of Kansas about 6,000 years after the last glacial retreat to complete the transformation from snow forest to scrubland to prairie, a process that took neighboring prairies such as the one that once covered Lincoln, Nebraska, where I now live, less than 200 years. In other words, prairie is outermost. It is the last evolved and will probably be the first dissolved, and the forests are merely trying to reclaim what was once theirs. Just another Alsace-Lorraine.

Though Gleason clearly identifies the sumac with the forest and sees the latter as making astonishing progress in its assault and invasion of the grasslands to the tune of a basketball court or so each season, Weaver's studies suggest that if Gleason had observed his sumac armies for a full rather than half century, he might not have found them so consistently triumphant. In one study in particular, Weaver observed five hundred square feet of thicket just a few miles north of Lincoln. Prairie cordgrass with its rough-edged leaves formed the lower border of the grove; pure prairie—probably big and little bluestems, though Weaver doesn't say—formed the upper edge. To halt the further expansion of the sumac frontier, the shrubs had been mown, but clearly the grasses needed no special reinforcements to defend their self-determined borders.

In 1924, the number of sumac shoots in the marginal area of uninvaded prairie was 174, seventy of which were new. Two years later, Weaver reports, the number of shoots had decreased by 28 percent. The 1927 figures prove that not only was the sumac making no progress up the slopes, it was actually losing ground against the unmown grasses. Moreover, the sumacs that did survive were flat-topped and small when compared to those sumacs near the moister ravine bottom. Weaver concluded that, contrary to what we might expect, one of the most aggressive members of the shrub community was unable to advance into true prairie.

Other studies conducted on the sumac thickets determined that the slow advance of chaparral and woodland was hastened during wet seasons and retarded during dry ones. During droughty periods, it even retreated. "It appears fairly certain that there can be no final victory for either," Weaver observed. "There can only be periods of varying duration in which prairie or forest holds ground won by the favor of the changing cycle." To my eye, a moving edge belongs more to the advancing than the receding side, but an edge as stable as the one Weaver observed, where what lies on either side contributes equally to the stasis, is clearly shared. Yet Weaver didn't see it that way. In *Prairie Plants and Their Environment* (1968) he wrote, "The fascinating problem of the relationship of the *forest edge* to the grassland has been much debated" (emphasis mine).

I can justify Weaver's identification of the sumac with the forest. Prairie historian James C. Malin labeled those Europeans and East Coasters who believed "good" land was wooded and humid as "forest men." Once they arrived in the trans-Missouri West, these newcomers described the land in terms of what it lacked: it was treeless and subhumid. As a result, the grasses that the prairies offered in such lush abundance and diversity were just so much negative space. After all, grasses weren't trees or wildflowers, and unlike such "real" plants, grasses thrived in abnormally dry conditions. When Lieutenant John C. Frémont led an exploratory expedition through the Platte River Valley to the South Pass in 1843, the "Great Pathfinder" recorded in his journal somewhere near Laramie that while his traveling companions were hunting buffalo and buffalo chips, "I amused myself with hunting plants among the grasses." According to Malin, it wasn't until Frémont's second trip west that he identified the short, tough patches of buffalo grass, and on neither trip did he reveal any acquaintance with the prevalent flag-shaped grama grasses. Grass was the backdrop against which real plants appeared—sage, false indigo, sunflowers, prairie potatoes. Though Weaver was born not in Europe nor on the East Coast but on the tallgrass prairie of Villisca, Iowa, and though he spent most of his life on the grasslands studying root systems in deep trenches and writing about the prairie as if its life depended on him, he is just as fickle about his borders as the rest of us. For no reason I can determine, other than individual preference or culturally conditioned response, Weaver saw the edge as part of the forest in spite of the presence of grasses he loved.

If we are "on edge," we are all cuts and angles: nervous, anxious, oversensitive ("The edginess in the presence of the actual world characterizes a great deal of transcendent metaphysics," reads an old column from *The Listener*). One who walks a razor's edge must be balanced, deliberate, alert. One who rides an edgy horse must be skilled or daring or stupid. One who approaches the fringe, where the unexpected lurks, should approach it "edgingly"—cautiously, mincingly, with barely perceptible steps—since to go "over the edge" is to be irretrievably lost. Edges are places most of us would rather not be.

In addition to the danger it presents, the edge is also undesirable because it is removed from the heart of the matter. To "edge" a tablecloth is to stitch lace or fringe not to the part of the cloth where we place the entree or centerpiece but to its less noticed perimeters. Paintings that are "edgy" are too much outline, not enough heart. An "edger" or fettler uses a knife or sponge to smooth not that part of the clay pot that will bear the showy pattern, but the plainer joints and seams. To "work the edges" of an idea, a territory, a power structure, is to work the outskirts with the hopes of moving inward. To get information "by the edges" is to get it imperfectly, by the hem of the garment instead of by the arm or the beating heart. And if we are "on edge," we are out of joint because we are too far from the still center. The ecologists are correct: the edge *is* a tension zone.

But, too, there is much about an edge that is desirable. It is not the broad of the blade, the scabbard, the handle, or even the point of the sword that convinces, but the edge. If a conversation edges us out, we take drastic measures and slide a word in "edgewise." To "have an edge on someone" is to be better or keener than that other ("Belle's got the edge on you," Rhett Butler told Scarlett O'Hara, "because she's a kind-hearted, good-natured soul"). To lose one's edge is lamentable: it is to peel potatoes with a butter knife instead of a paring knife.

"Dangers . . . give the same edge to life here that the mountains give to the horizon," Hart Crane wrote in a 1932 letter. Because of this inherent power and danger, those who exist on the cutting edge—that ragged line where sky and mountain meet, that trembling rim at the outermost limit of the expected or the accepted—possess a terrible beauty. They are the trailblazers who lead the rest of us onto unfamiliar ground . . . or cause us to root ourselves even more deeply in the safe and the familiar.

Mostly, edges are mixed blessings.

I appreciate an edge that is wide enough to name. The mayfly spends all but a few days of her life underwater, breathing through gills and scuttering beneath stones. Then she climbs onto a rock or branch at the water's edge, where she sheds her skin and unfurls smoky, impotent wings. One more molt, and presto chango, she is a clear-winged adult who leaves her rock once and for all, to hover over land in a brown, concupiscent cloud of Ephemeroptera. Entomologists have named that one-day period between naiad and fly "subimago," meaning the stage immediately before the final, reproductive adult stage or "imago." But this name identifies the flightless, winged creature as more one thing than another, when what she needs is a name that describes her one-day edge as neither water bug nor fly but as separate from both or equally related to both. Thresholder. Edge-dweller. Neither-nor bug. Nonetheless, the mayfly life cycle possesses clean, identifiable edges: first molt, dun; second molt, spinner.

But edges aren't always this neat. Go back in time twenty or thirty years and drive Bluff Road, a curving highway that hugged the bluffs in my Mississippi River hometown. When I was a child the road was a narrow, two-lane highway. The eastern edge was but a slim shoulder bordered by cement posts strung with cables, after which it was a precipitous fall to the river bottoms. The western edge of the highway was a sharp, exposed bluff where a sign warned, DANGER! FALLING ROCKS. Study the sedimentary layers in the bluff and you will see that they are not neat affairs like layers of a strawberry tort, rings on a tree stump, or the hard-edged rectangles of geologic periods, eras and epochs stacked one upon another in the encyclopedia. The lines the earth draws are prone to exceptions like the waving layers of solidified liquid in motion that formed the tall bluff. Thus, you are likely to find a little Silurian eruption in your Devonian layer; a Cretaceous dip or two in your Jurassic. The type of line any drunkard would prefer to walk.

Some edges are even messier. Most prairie ecologists identify three distinct grassland formations: tallgrass, which extends from east central Nebraska to the edge of the eastern deciduous forest; the shortgrass prairie, which extends from the Nebraska Panhandle to the foot of the Rockies; and a swath of mixed grasses between the two.

But where and how prairie ecologists draw the line between tall and mixed prairie varies. J. Richard Carpenter characterized tallgrass prairie as big and little bluestems, bison and wolves, mixed-grass prairie as grama grasses, bison and pronghorn antelopes. J. H. Schaffner, however, insisted that tallgrass ended where it met the eastern range of the harvester ant and the prairie dog. Given the tendency of some organisms to change their addresses in response to fluctuations in climate, food supply and predator-prey ratio, Carpenter's and Schaffner's boundaries are moving things. In contrast to both of these views, University of Nebraska botanist Frederick E. Clements and his colleagues (Weaver included) maintained that there was no tallgrass—mixed-grass border over which to haggle and split grasses, because there was no mixed-grass prairie. Rather, it was a "disclimax" of the eastern prairie, and if it weren't for the disruptive influences of fires, rodents, overgrazing, and agriculture, the two would be one.

No matter how one distinguishes the tall- and mixed-grass regions, if indeed one does, it is well nigh impossible to draw a line of demarcation between them that is as indisputable as the barbed wire fence parting national park and private rangeland. The best maps of North American grasslands acknowledge this impossibility by indicating prairie types with dots, *x*'s, and slashes, and by permitting those patterns to bulge and recede as if poured instead of drawn. Yet, even that is not adequate. Moisture in the soil varies greatly within a short distance, say, from the top to the bottom of a hill. Where the moisture varies so, too, does the vegetation. Malin explains that in tallgrass prairie, big and little bluestems grow on the dry, sandy uplands, but in mixed prairie, the same grasses grow on the slope, one step down, one step closer to the moisture. So, too, the big bluestem, which dominates the slopes in tallgrass prairie, grows in the moister lowlands on mixed grass. The tallest grasses of the true prairie, cord and switch, drop out completely in the transition because there is no place moist enough for them to plumb their thickly matted roots.

So where now shall we draw the boundary between the prairie types? Shall we be utterly meticulous and represent the hopscotch of vegetation on every single declivity or do we accept inaccurate generalizations—an overlap of dots and *x*'s, a blending of the yellow and blue zones, yellow-green here, blue-green there?

Gleason says that the environmental changes that form the boundaries between plant communities on a hillside are as effective in keeping each plant species within its own restricted area as a woven wire fence is in keeping chickens in the chicken yard. I can roughly determine where the sumac ends and grassland begins but am uncertain as to how to classify those upstarts that have jumped the fence. Are they the exceptions to the rule or do they form the outermost boundary of the encroaching forest?

I draw a line with a sharp pencil along the edge of a ruler and examine it under a magnifying lens. The edge I've drawn is more like that of the Missouri River border between Iowa and Nebraska—all eruptions, indentations, and equivocations—than it is like the straight and clean black line on the map separating Nebraska from Kansas. How much less shall I expect of edges drawn in air by the mind, an entity whose outermost boundaries are yet to be decided? (Does mind, for instance, end where the skull begins? Is mind contained in retina, eardrum, tongue tip, palm, and spine and so its boundaries are found in the miles of cell membranes one produces in a lifetime? Or is mind even greater than the outermost boundaries of the physical body, permitting one to become for a moment whatever objects she beholds?)

In Europe, the frontier was a fortified political boundary, drawn in metal and stone between two often densely populated regions. In nineteenth-century America, however, the frontier was a mind-drawn edge even less definite than the shifting natural border between tall- and mixed-grass prairies. Moreover, great significance was attached to this faintly drawn line, defined in the census reports as the margin of settlement (white man's, of course) with a density of two or more white people to the square mile. The frontier was as historian Frederick Jackson Turner variously called it, the "hither edge of free land"; the meeting point between "savagery and civilization"; the line of most "rapid and effective Americanization"; the outermost edge of Europe.

The frontier was the product of a repeated evolutionary process. Stand at the Cumberland Gap, Turner advised, or at the South Pass a century later, and you could witness "the progression of civilization marching single file . . . the fur-trader and hunter, the cattle raiser, the pioneer farmer—and the frontier had passed." Each successive wave of invaders worked the soil, making conditions more hospitable for those who followed, so in a real sense, frontier was that edge where other was converted into we and me, wilderness and "savagery" into shops and schoolmarms and the "New World" version of democracy, tall-grass into forest.

But at the 1893 meeting of the American Historical Association at the Chicago World's Columbian Exposition, Turner declared the frontier dead. To support his conclusion, he referred to the superintendent of the census, who said that up to and including 1880, the United States still had a frontier, but by 1890 the unsettled area "was so broken into by isolated bodies of settlement that the frontier line was no longer traceable" and thus existed only in the history books or in the imagination.

While Turner was convinced that the presence of "un-won wilderness" was responsible for the most striking characteristics of the American intellect ("that coarseness and strength combined with acuteness and inquisitiveness; that practical, inventive turn of mind, quick to find expedients; that masterful grasp of material things, lacking in the artistic but powerful to effect great ends; that restless, nervous energy; that dominant individualism, working for good and for evil, and withal that buoyancy and exuberance which comes with freedom— these are traits of the frontier, or traits called out elsewhere because of the existence of the frontier"), he was no rash prophet, declaring the expansive character of American life to have died with the physical frontier.

"Movement has been its dominant fact, and unless this training has no effect

upon a people," Turner predicted, "the American energy will continually demand a wider field for its exercise." But where, at the quincentenary of Columbus's arrival in the Caribbean, does the frontier now lie? After all, no unmapped continents, rivers, or mountains remain to be named or renamed after
oneself or one's ruler. Neither are there enough unfathomed oceanic mountain
ranges to satisfy all of humankind's frontiering desires. Other planets and solar
systems are too far-flung from the known edge of our world for us to hurl ourselves toward them. Now, our choice is either to permit our frontiering im-
pulses to wither and turn to dust or to divert them toward other fulfillment.

Turner did not limit the frontier to a physical place. In his 1910 address "Social Forces in American History," he noted that because America was in the
process of "readjusting its old ideals to new conditions [it is] turning increas-
ingly to government to preserve its traditional democracy." What had once
been centers of pioneer democracy were in Turner's time the setting for social-
istic reforms—new political parties, the demand for primary elections, ini-
tiative referendum, recall, and so forth—all "efforts to find substitutes for
that safe-guard of democracy, the disappearing free lands." Turner concludes
that after the physical edge between claimed and unclaimed disappeared, the
American frontier became that place where "the bonds of custom are broken
and unrestraint is triumphant."

A place of unbounded possibilities.

The heart is the most vital portion, the most intense and concentrated expression of an entity, the part nearest the middle. Thus, the heart of the country,
an oak tree, a cabbage, or a message possesses a single and undiluted energy.

Yet people rarely live on their holiest grounds. Rather, they live along the
periphery, make pilgrimages into the powerful center, and then return to
the equally powerful edge, where two fields—secular and profane, wild and
tame—are for a hair-fine moment inseparable. The testimonies of edge-
dwellers confirm the power of two forces commingled in a single space.

"I was born in the in-between," says novelist and poet Leslie Marmon Silko,
who believes that her 1948 birth date places her between the old generation,
which remembers Wounded Knee, and the post–World War II generation,
which does not. "I understand why the old folks cry, and don't understand why
they have to keep burying. You know, I'm in a strange place," she concludes.
Since Silko's ancestry is Anglo, Laguna, and Mexican, she is not fully a part of
any one culture, yet writes insightfully of all three. Neither is her individual
identity always clear: sometimes she is herself; sometimes she is one of her creations; sometimes she is a blend of the two. After reviewing the transcripts of

an interview with Laura Coltelli, author of *Winged Words: American Indian Writers Speak* (1990), for instance, Silko wrote that she was horrified to see "how crude and convoluted and wild" her comments were, but understood why that was: in the process of writing *Almanac of the Dead*, "my subconscious cannibalized this interview to create an important character, I call Angelita. I realized now I could not edit or salvage this interview because the character called Angelita had already taken possession of all my notions and ideas. . . . The novel is a voracious feeder upon the psyche."

Those who teeter on the edge are in a position to see the substance of the adjacent regions more clearly and honestly than those deeply rooted in the interior. As anthropologist Walter Goldschmidt observed, it is the gap between our own culturally conditioned worldview and that of another with a radically different orientation that offers us a glimpse of the world as it really is . . . a condition worth cultivating. "It would be some advantage to live a primitive and frontier life," wrote Henry David Thoreau, "though in the midst of an outward civilization, if only to learn what are the gross necessities of life." Thus the new citizen, the political prisoner, the assembly-line worker turned street person, the terminally ill can tell us more about both sides of the line between justice and injustice, freedom and restraint, goodness and malevolence, life and death than can one who has yet to discover the outer reaches of her own mind, her own life, her own loyalties, her own backyard.

How you describe a drinking glass in which the water rests at the mid-point between the top and the bottom supposedly reveals whether you are an optimist (the glass is half full) or a pessimist (the glass is half empty). While these answers may provide a superficial sketch of one's psyche, they fail to describe accurately the condition of the tumbler: it is neither half full nor half empty, but both. Water and space meet mid-line.

The fatal flaw of Frederick Jackson Turner's theory is not his monocausationist view of American history, as many of his critics contend, but that he did not understand that every edge is a double-edged sword with the potential to cut in either direction. Moreover, substance lies on both sides of the edge, not just on one.

The American frontier was the westward-moving line of encounter between the continent's first human inhabitants and those more recently arrived, between old and new land claims, between town and forest, farm and prairie. The glory and the horror of the American frontier was that it destroyed as it created. In his failure to speak of what it was like to face instead of to follow the cutting edge, Turner told only half the story, and no history of this continent is

complete without accounts from those on both sides of the edge: the posses-
sors and the dispossessed. In his failure to tell the whole story, Turner proved
himself just as unwilling to break new ground as his colleagues were.

I watch my son fit together a hundred-piece puzzle of an idyllic street in Ger-
many. He fits the last piece, a chunk of gray cobblestone snuggled against the
red wheel of a flower cart. I study the completed picture. I take away the wheel
and the street has the edge; I take away the chunk of street and the wheel has
the edge. If I owned a flower cart, I might find it more natural to speak of the
edge of the wheel, though if I were in the cobblestone business, I would more
likely speak of the edge of the street. However, I neither peddle nor pave, so I
identify more completely with the seen flower vendor and his bright props than
the unseen mason from centuries ago. Yet the puzzle will not permit such prej-
udiced vision: its edges are conspicuously shared and cannot be ignored.

I go to the sumac thicket. All I see is part of an enormous jigsaw puzzle. Instead of a pastry shop, street musicians, hotel, flower cart, and cobblestone
street, my pieces are brown bunchgrasses and dried composite seedheads, a
wooded creek, a ribbon of burning bushes, widely spaced cumulus clouds, a
drifting hawk, big sky. Where two pieces meet, say blue sky and a red turkey-
footed seed stalk, a single line is formed. The familiar big bluestem tries to persuade me that the edge belongs to it, but I will not be moved.

I study a small sumac on the edge of the thicket nearest the prairie. A serrated edge lies between red leaf and blue sky; a rough edge between brown
stalk and sky; a scalloped edge between upright velvety red berries and sky.
The edge makes sense of substance and space as it outlines leaf and sky, since
perception of figure depends, above all, upon the existence of an edge. Ironically, it is at that point where something is least itself and most inseparable
from the other—waxing and waning civilizations, new idea and old, one biome
and the next, leaflet and sky—that it also receives its form, its definition, its
identity . . . that which makes it most itself.

Fall 1992

# HOUSEGUEST

~~~~~~~~~~~~~~~~

*I* was in bed, reading, about ready to drift off to sleep, when I heard it: *cree-cree, cree-cree, cree-cree.* Perhaps my daughter was still awake and I was hearing the bell on her train. I returned to my book. But there it was again: *cree-cree, cree-cree, cree-cree.* I realized it wasn't a Fisher-Price toy I was hearing, but a cricket's stridulations, the sounds produced when a cricket rubs the sharp edge of one front wing along a filelike ridge beneath the other front wing. It didn't matter whether it was a house or field cricket I was hearing. Any cricket in the house meant a poor night's sleep.

I'd had uninvited houseguests of this nature before. If I was to sleep, I'd have to find the culprit and release him into my backyard, where he could sing to his heart's content. But I knew better than to look for my guest. There were literally hundreds of hiding places, including the baseboards, my wool sweaters and blazers, and the stack of magazines and books by my bed. Searching for this pest would be futile. I turned my air filter on high, hoping that the white noise would cover the stridulations. It did not. Eventually, I carried my pillow and blanket to the quiet of my study and slept on the floor.

I bring the outside in. In my study, cut birch boughs lean against the wall, their black eyes always half closed. On my desk sits a basket filled with enough acorns to start a small oak grove, with no two trees of the same species. In another basket are jumbled the feathers of finches, orioles, hawks, geese, blue jays, cardinals, owls, and flamingos. In a vase rise dried stalks of sedges, big bluestem, switchgrass, and wild rye. Lining the forefront of my bookshelves are rocks, shells, fossils, and bones. Lately I've been yearning for an ant farm, which I would set on a table near my computer. Then when I tire of watching tiny black forms moving across my screen, I could watch tiny black forms moving through tunnels in the sand.

Guests from the natural world who are either dead (though not decaying) or invited are welcome in my home. The cricket in my bedroom is neither.

The second night, I heard the chirping before I even got into bed. Perhaps the room was too hot. I read that the speed of the stridulations rises at a very predictable rate in relation to the temperature. In fact, you can rather accurately determine the temperature by adding forty to the number of chirps you hear in a fifteen-second interval. I turned down the heat, figuring I could at least decrease the frequency of the cricket's song.

Only males sing, though both sexes have stridulating organs. If female crickets have been my guests in the past, their presence was beyond my ken. So too, the male cricket's courtship song, which is a continuous trill in the ultrasonic range, too high for my ears to hear. I am grateful that I am sensible of only a fraction of the cricket activity that might be taking place in my home.

But why do I appreciate the cricket's coarse call when I hear it in my backyard yet find it a nuisance when it is trapped in my house? What type of nature lover am I? One who wants to assign nature to a separate sphere that I can freely enter and exit. One who wants the natural world to enter my domain only when invited. A nature lover with a double standard.

The old saw says that dirty laundry and houseguests start stinking after three days and should be gotten rid of. But another old saw says if you can't change the situation, change your attitude. On the third night of the cricket's visit, I heeded the advice of the latter. For my bedtime reading material I chose *The*

*Insect World of J. Henri Fabre.* If anyone could change my attitude about the cricket, it would be the great French entomologist.

Fabre (1823–1915) began his career as a science teacher but was fired for permitting female students in his classes. For the next decade he wrote popular science books for children, an occupation that barely met his family's financial needs. All the while he dreamed of owning a small plot of land where he could study insects. When Fabre was fifty-five, his dream came true: he had saved enough money to buy a *harmas*, 2.7 acres of sunbaked land unfit for farming or grazing but ideal for his entomological studies. In his "laboratory of the open fields," the man whom Charles Darwin called an "incomparable observer" patiently observed and recorded the finest details of the daily lives of spiders, grasshoppers, glowworms, scorpions, beetles, and caterpillars. That Fabre studied the *living* insect in its natural habitat is especially remarkable, since most other naturalists of his time were preoccupied with the pinned specimen and consequently knew little of insect behavior. Because Fabre wrote so extensively and poetically of insect lives, he was known as "the insect's Homer." His ten-volume, 2,500-page *Souvenirs Entomologiques* was a fifty-five-year labor of love, for which the French government rewarded him with a $400 annual pension and the Legion of Honor ribbon.

While Fabre was usually outside, waiting in a ravine for hunting wasps or studying thistle weevils at night by the light of his lantern, he was also able to study insects in his home, since whatever lived outside was welcome within. "Bolder still, the Wasp has taken possession of the dwelling-house," Fabre writes in *The Life of the Grasshopper*. "On my door-sill, in a soil of rubbish, nestles the white-banded Sphex: when I go indoors, I must be careful not to damage her burrows, not to tread upon the miner absorbed in her work." Fabre called his *harmas* "Eden," a place where all creatures are guests and no one is host. No double standard there.

Fabre invited crickets into his home, too. Each day he made "assiduous visits" to pairs of crickets he had isolated and caged until he observed the females ovipositing. Fabre dug up their eggs and brought them home in an earth-filled pot. Weeks later, the five thousand to six thousand eggs hatched. In time, Fabre's house pulsed with cricket music, "first in rare and shy solos, soon developing into a general symphony." Their song was "monotonous and artless, but so well-suited, in its very crudity, to the rustic gladness of renascent life! It is the hosanna of the awakening, the sacred alleluia understood by the swelling seed and sprouting blade. . . . Were the Lark to fall silent, the fields blue-grey with lavender, swinging its fragrant censors before the sun, would still receive from this humble chorister a solemn celebration."

An alleluia, indeed. Fabre was able to hear something sacred and celebratory in the cricket's song because insects were his raison d'être. The cricket was an annoyance to me. I listened again to my houseguest's song. Joyous, yes. Hosanna, perhaps. I drifted off to sleep.

The fourth night, I waited. No chirping. I turned up the heat. Nothing. Though the room was quiet and I was tired, I read very late.

My guest had taken his leave, one way or another. I read that one acre of prairie can support up to ten thousand crickets, with each adult eating three-fourths its own body weight per day. While my half-acre backyard hadn't the fodder of tallgrass prairie, it could at least host several hundred crickets. Perhaps the cricket in my bedroom had rejoined the feast and the symphony in my backyard.

But not *my* backyard. Crickets ate grass, seeds, and bugs, scraped their fiddles, laid their eggs, and were eaten by meadowlarks and nighthawks on this land long before my kind arrived. My cement patio and driveway, my chain-link fence, and my not-so-well-sealed house are but recent interruptions on this millennia-old cricket field. The multitude of crickets are my hosts; I am but an uninvited guest.

May 1995

# EXCAVATIONS

Among my Daily-Papers, which I bestow on the Publick,
there are some which are written with Regularity and
Method, and others that run out into the Wildness of those
Compositions, which go by the Name of Essays. . . . As for
the first, I have the whole Scheme of the Discourse in Mind,
before I set Pen to Paper. In the other kind of Writing, it
is sufficient that I have several Thoughts on the Subject,
without troubling myself to range them in order, that they
may seem to grow out of one another, and be disposed under
the proper Heads.
JOSEPH ADDISON, *Spectator*, no. 476,
Friday, September 4, 1712

*I*t was a walk that had already yielded plenty. I had ventured far enough
from the road to stand on the shore of a lake of ferns, each cupped heavenward like a satellite dish. I'd weighted my cardigan pockets with flinty gray-
and-white-striped rocks. I'd sloshed through a soggy ditch beneath eight-foot-
tall reeds—part cattail, part tasseled corn—where I found the frogs I'd been
hearing. I'd studied grasshoppers that bore little resemblance to the green 'hop-
pers I'd chased in Iowa meadows as a child and held in my clasped palms until
they spit tobacco. Vermont grasshoppers are black, gold, brown, and winged,
and I couldn't persuade them to spit for anything.

But then, on the gravel shoulder, I found a dun, mouselike creature, dead,
curled in a fetal position. It was a mouse with a snout, but no mere pig's snout:

this was a proboscis with a flair. It was piggish with two nostrils near the center, but from the outer rim sprouted fingers of pink flesh like the spokes of a rimless wheel, the petals of a sunflower, or the tentacles of a branching idea.

This was too much to trust to my memory, so I broke my rule of leaving wild things—even dead wild things—at peace, rolled the corpse onto a Kleenex with a twig, and carried it home. Once there, I laid it on my desk and sketched its fabulous nose in my notebook. Then I sketched its entirety with words: "A dun, mouselike creature, dead, curled in a fetal position."

Since I hadn't anticipated the need for a spade or shovel when I packed for my week and a half in Vermont, once my notebook was full, I flushed the creature down the toilet—the most respectable burial I could give under the circumstances.

For nature essayists, the subjects for our excavations fall at our feet like bread rained from heaven. A dead opossum. A flushed pheasant. An approaching cloud of mayflies. Bare branches studded with white-headed eagles. Consequently, when I was stopped short by a dead mole on the road, I knew I would write about her, though I didn't know what I would write. Other gifts presented me with an angle, a handle, a purpose as soon as I beheld them. While driving back to Nebraska from Vermont, for instance, I was startled by a great blue heron standing stock-still near a farm pond in the midst of a moving landscape so close to Interstate 80 that I questioned my own ability to see and name. In September, I had eyes only for flaming groves of sumac and spent all autumn reading and writing about their border existence while carrying sprigs of dried purple berries in my buttonhole. Next, two failed attempts at autobiographical essays, which, above all, reminded me why I need to write about other living things than myself (more timely and timeless, less self-indulgent, more downright interesting). Then, one January morning, it happened. I woke up, as I always do, with the desire to write, but on that day I had no subject matter. No circle of hell could be worse. So, I resurrected the mole.

Still, I wasn't ready to write, since I hadn't a slant on my subject. Though I was half a continent, half a year away from that August afternoon in Vermont when I found the mole's body, I was no closer, no further from making an essay about her than I had been. I knew if I didn't find some way to write about her, I'd turn her now warm body over and over in my mind in the middle of the night, fretting myself sleepless until I found an angle, a handle, a purpose. So, I did the next best thing to writing about the star-nosed mole: I went to the library and read about her.

Most of the facts I read—and the metaphors I glimpsed—pertained to the *Condylura cristata*'s two farthest ends: the tip of her blooming nose and what I discovered to be her not-so-ratlike tail. I learned that her nose (which I had not noted in such fine detail) comprised exactly and always (barring accidents) twenty-two pink flesh rays or tentacles, one-quarter to one-half inch long. These are arranged symmetrically, eleven on each side, the two topmost rays held rigidly forward while the others move continually in the mole's search for food. Once she nabs a succulent earthworm with her shovel feet, she removes all distractions by retracting her rays so she can work, chewing down the length of the worm as if it were spaghetti. A nose with table manners.

While mole experts Terry Yates and Richard Pedersen claim the exact function of the nasal rays isn't yet known, it's apparent that this nose, like the weird snout of the anteater, the tapir, or the elephant, is a highly specialized sensory device. Each of the twenty-two rays, in fact, is covered with papillae (David Van Vleck saw fifteen to twenty on just the base of a single ray under low magnification), and each papilla bears one to three sensory organs named after Theodor Eimer, the German scientist who "discovered" them in 1871. This means that the mole's pointed nose isn't an earthmover as we might expect (the feet do that) but a sensitive instrument that directs the forepaws in their work. The nose is the locator of the mole's prey and her position in the world.

Almost as interesting as the mole's remarkable nose is her tail. In August, it looks like that of a rat or mouse: a long whip about half the length of the creature's body from tentacle tip to tail base. But in the winter or early spring, that tail is quite a different story. Then it is constricted near the base, swollen with stored fat near the middle like that of a snake that has just swallowed a bowl of mush. Most swollen tails are as big around as a number two lead pencil, some are as large in cross-section as a dime, and curiously, some tails never swell.

Apparently, moles use the stored fat during breeding season or at other times when their food intake cannot meet their energy requirements. William Robert Eadie and William John Hamilton learned that the great majority of star-nosed moles of both sexes had swollen tails before and during breeding season, but once the season was over, their tails were ratlike again. In addition to acting as a portable pantry, this tail functions as an antenna of sorts. In his study of the European mole, Godet states that the characteristically erect tail acts as an organ of touch, maintaining contact with the roof of the tunnels rather like the overhead pickup of an electric train.

Other noteworthy facts about *Condylura cristata*—Weight: three ounces. Length: six inches. Habits: diurnal, nocturnal, active year-round. Preferred habitat: damp, boggy soil near streams or in swamps and meadows in New England and southeastern Canada. Food: insects, worms, small fish, vegetable matter. Tunnels: deep and permanent where nests are built; shallow surface runways where food is gotten. Breeding: one litter per year of two to five molelets (my own terminology, I believe). Since other small mammals produce three to four litters per year, the mole's low replacement rate suggests few predators: an occasional hawk, owl, skunk, fox, coyote, snake, raccoon, cat, dog, big fish, or golf course owner.

Joseph Wood Krutch says that to the essayist a fact is "at best a peg to hang something on." A typewritten page and a half of facts about the secret life of the mole takes me only a little closer to an essay about her than I was before. Now I have pegs. But what shall I hang upon them?

Some facts are so taut and humming, I could hang on to their tails and be carried into the heart of an essay. Consider this simple fact from Victor H. Cahalane: "Few people have ever seen a mole." Not exactly an earth-moving revelation until I add it to the following list: few people have ever seen a miracle, the heart of darkness, an exploding star, or birds mating in midair. Therein lies the focus and the motive for an essay about a mole: why and how those of us who have witnessed the extraordinary should communicate our experience to those who haven't.

Julian of Norwich, an essayist of sorts, received sixteen "shewings" or revelations of divine love during her thirtieth year while on what she and others believed to be her deathbed. Julian survived, but had no other revelations and so spent the rest of her anchored days writing and revising the substance of that one extraordinary night: ". . . and truly charity urgeth me to tell you of it," she confessed. The nature essayist's reason for witnessing is often more mundane than soul salvation. Michel-Guillaume-Jean de Crèvecoeur, for instance, observed two snakes engaged in mortal battle, their necks wrapped twice around each other's, their tails lashed around hemp stalks to obtain greater leverage so it appeared that the two stalks were playing tug-of-war with the twined reptiles. Crèvecoeur felt compelled to relate the anecdote simply because the circumstances were "as true as they are singular."

Another fact, another promise of an essay: "Relatively speaking," write Yates and Pedersen, "little is known scientifically of these mammals. . . . Moles are probably the least understood major component of the North American mammalian fauna." Even though we've lost our hankering for moleskin caps and purses, even though tiny baked moles don't grace our tables as do tiny baked quails, and never do moles make good house pets, rarely living a year in captivity and requiring dirt and worms and all, nonetheless we should be interested in any creature capable of moving our foundation. Because moles sometimes eat what we've planted or move the soil away from it, we've devoted more attention to their eating habits and how best to exterminate them from our lawns than any other aspect of their biology. Still, there's more to the mole than what she does and does not eat.

This assertion leads me to speculate about how much else is so unstudied. Once I read that approximately seven hundred arachnid species have yet to be discovered. Initially, my fascination with this statistic lay in that so much remained to be named in a world chin-deep in nouns—common, proper, colloquial, scientific, vulgar, euphemistic, and so forth. But then I began wondering how such a fantastic and unsubstantiated figure was reached. In other words, how could anyone even roughly estimate the breadth of what she does not know? Do experts in all fields—archeology, astronomy, linguistics, music theory—possess similar statistics about their respective unknowns?

If the mole is so unstudied, I suspect there is an entire essay on the curious few who *have* made her their lifework. Eimer, for instance, the first person known to have studied the star-nosed mole's "schnozz." Or Eadie, who researched everything from skin gland activity and pelage differences to male accessory reproductive glands and unique prostatic secretions. What type of passion and audacity does such lifework demand? A little biography could reveal a lot not only about those who study moles but about any naturalist with an all-consuming passion. After all, I suppose the moody, aristocratic John James Audubon is wilder and rarer than any of the birds and mammals whose biographies he wrote. Second-generation violaphile Viola Brainerd Baird, scaling Mount Olympus in search of a rare violet species or raising hybrids to maturity with her father, Ezra Brainerd (husband of Francis Viola), delights me more than any of the careful paintings and descriptions in her *Wild Violets of North America* (1942). So, too, Charles Darwin's final work, *The Formation of Vegetable Mould, Through the Actions of Worms, With Observation of Their Habits* (1881), leaves me more intrigued with the habits of this particular scientist (he shined a bull-lantern in the worms' eyes to determine if they could see; he chewed a plug of tobacco near their noses to test their sense of smell; he placed their earth-filled pots on his piano and banged away to see if they could hear) than it does about the humus-creating annelids. Darwin suspected that readers would be much more interested in his theory that humans "descended" than they would be in how worms had formed the rich topsoil in which humans planted their crops and so, in an addendum to his autobiography, he apologized: "This is a subject of small importance; and I know not whether it will interest any reader, but it has interested me." An essay about those who shun the popular and profitable for that of seemingly small importance is an essay I want to write; it is an essay I want to read.

Though little is known of the mole, the few passionate researchers who have excavated her hidden life have provided enough facts to refute widely held misconceptions. (If these assumptions cloud our ability to see the mole as she really is, then this essay could be another meditation on the same earlier fact: "Few people have ever seen a mole.") "Looking at the mole, we would expect the animal to be rather slow and somewhat methodical," observed Richard Headstrom. "But surprisingly, the speed with which it can tunnel through the earth is almost incredible." Headstrom reports that the star-nosed mole has been clocked tunneling a distance of 235 feet in a single night. This is comparable to an average-sized woman digging a 2,500-foot tunnel at least wide enough for her body to pass through in one night. How much else do we incorrectly assume about the mole? (At this point, I expect an essay full of appearances and realities.) For instance, I expected the mole to wear a ratty, mangy coat, living in dirt and leaf-litter nests the way she does, but I've observed that her coat is velvety soft, the hairs lying smoothly and willingly in either direction. While I would expect her to be nearly deaf, since her outer ear is all but invisible, the structures of the middle and inner ears are relatively large; therefore, her hearing may be quite keen. Neither is the mole mute. Gillian Godfrey and Peter Crowcroft report that moles emit at least two sounds distinguishable by the human ear: "a soft twittering made when feeding or exploring, and loud squeaks made singly or in succession when fighting." Because the mole's nasal passages are longer than those of most other animals, we would expect her snout to be extraordinarily sensitive, able to smell an earthworm at fifty paces, but it is not. The nose *is* sensitive, but as a feeler, not as a sniffer. Finally, because the mole has few predators to escape and breeds so seldom (once a year, three-year life span), we might expect her to sleep her life away, since there is so little to stay awake for. But in truth, the mole works around the clock, snatching sleep only occasionally. Because she works so much and has such a fast metabolism, she must eat one-third to one-half her body weight in food each day just to stay alive. Imagine how many waking hours it would require for an average-sized woman to eat forty to sixty pounds of food per day. So, too, the mole. At this point, my essay about appearances and realities could take a sharp, argumentative turn and persuade the reader to elect the industrious, sensitive, unassuming mole as our national symbol instead of the lazy, thieving fish vulture.

The same topic of appearance and reality approached from another direction: how different mammalogists reach different conclusions about similar data. In 1927, Fred Stevens of Ithaca, New York, presented William John Hamilton, Jr., of Cornell University with a male and female *Condylura* (the female was not pregnant), which Stevens had taken from the same minnow trap. Hamilton offered two interpretations for the presence of two moles in the same place: either they were together for an early courtship prior to mating or they exhibited a tendency for companionship. Hamilton places more weight on the latter, concluding that the star-nosed mole is not only gregarious but colonial. Victor Cahalane's position is more moderate. While no mole will ever win a congeniality award, the star-nosed and the hairy-tailed are more tolerant of their kind than are other mole species. Moreover, it is not uncommon for them to use a community system of runways. Yates and Pedersen agree that moles may be found together but believe that this curiosity relates more to food supply than to need for companionship. Similarly, Leonard Lee Rue III portrays the star-nosed as a recluse. "Although this species is more sociable than the common mole, most moles lead a solitary existence. Only rarely are several moles found inhabiting the same tunnel, and these usually are females and their young of the year. The female does not tolerate the male after breeding, but raises her family by herself." Colonial? Together out of necessity? Hermits? I am curious about how the mammalogist's own attitudes toward companionship and solitude influence his reading of the mole's behavior. "What we observe is not nature itself," says Werner Heisenberg, "but nature exposed to our method of questioning." What questions were each of these scientists asking about the mole? What questions am I asking about the mole and those who study her?

At this point, I pause to reread what I've written. I am struck by my own metaphorical loose ends. In paragraph five, I state that the mole is like the subject of an essay ("For nature essayists, the subjects for our excavations fall at our feet like bread rained from heaven"), which is to say that our subjects are at the same time sought, uncovered, and sometimes brought forth; prayed for, waited upon, and sometimes received. The metaphor is accurate if you can forget where moles come from. A few paragraphs later, I suggest that the movements of moles and essayists in their search for prey or their way in the world are each guided by a felt or intuitive sense. A few pages later, I say that the essayist's method is like the method of those who devote themselves to studying the homely form of the mole instead of something more glamorous (wolves, cranes, whales), involving more exciting methods of discovery (dog-sleds, blinds, wet suits) in exotic parts of the globe (Siberia, Japan, California). Not all mammalogists, not all essayists have to leave home to find their subject matter: just this week, I've seen three common Eastern moles within blocks of my house.

Too, I am struck by my reliance on metaphor to reveal the act of essaying. But this is fitting. Trying to capture the essay or the act of essaying in words is like "trying to catch a fish in the open hand," says Elizabeth Hardwick. The essay is too protean, too slippery, too edgeless for definitions and parameters.

The only recourse is to capture it partially through metaphors or, better, to demonstrate essaying in an essay that doubles back on itself, self-consciously reflecting on the method that produced it.

Which leads me to my next topic: an essay whose sole subject is form—an essay about preliminaries. The star-nosed mole introduces herself fringed nose first, typically tubular body next, and barometric tail last. Other creaturely introductions include: hard, toothless seed case crackers; fatty, velvety, neighing muzzles; rooting, rip-snorting snouts; twitching pink buttons; neat reptilian pinpricks; sharp-pointed bloodsuckers. Like the introduction to an essay, noses usually precede the body, even if only by a nose. Like any first impression, they can be deceptive (the remainder of the star-nosed mole is quite dull compared to his elaborate fanfare). Just as an introduction only positions the essayist for her excavations, the dinner guests for the meat of the conversation, the mole's nose only locates the place where the feet will begin digging. My essay about introductions would not only explain their similarity to noses but would itself be a series of positionings. An essay that is pure preface. An essay that introduces nothing. An essay, like this one, that never leaves the ground.

If the mole's nose is like an introduction, perhaps the body of the mole's work is like the body of the essayist's work. (Or different than.) An extended analogy could shed light on the dark burrowings of both. Again, the facts speak. While excavating, the mole uses every last hair and muscle. She turns her body forty-five degrees to the right if she is pushing dirt with her left forepaw, forty-five degrees to the left if she is pushing dirt with her right spade. Thus, she creates a back-and-forth spiraling motion like that of an electric borer. Nature essayist Richard Rhodes identifies the spiral rather than the circle or line as the movement of the essay itself, and for this reason, he says the essay is the most extemporaneous written form, and by definition, always unfinished.

Just as snow plowed from the road has to go someplace, so, too, the shoveled earth. When constructing deep tunnels, the mole throws the loosened soil under and back, then uses her hind feet to kick it to the rear. When a load has accumulated, she literally somersaults, then pushes the dirt ahead until it spills out, forming the mountain we call a molehill. From the upstairs window we can imagine or deduce the process that produced the pattern just as surely as the best essays bear hints of the process that produced them. But when the mole tunnels near the surface, evidence remains that leaves nothing to the imagination—soft raised ridges wrinkle the lawn or pasture. One reading tells it all.

The essay's path is cut not with big clawed feet but through "the act of thinking things out, feeling and finding a way; it is the mind in the marvels and miseries of its making, in the *work* of the imagination, the search for form," as William Gass observes. The essayist's cutting claws are also the words she chooses. In *The Writing Life*, Annie Dillard explains: "The line of words is a miner's pick, a woodcarver's gouge, a surgeon's probe. You wield it, and it digs a path you follow. Soon you find yourself in a new territory. . . . You make the path boldly and follow it fearfully. You go where the path leads."

Not so different from the way the mole works. "Apparently, it digs wherever fancy or food takes it without thought of any definite plan, so that ultimately it ends up with an intricate system of many-branched tunnels," Headstrom observes. Zoologist David Van Vleck terms it the "hit-or-miss path of the mole." While a rare essayist such as John McPhee cuts a certain path ("I want to get the structural problems out of the way first, so I can get to what matters more . . . the story"), most essayists set out "with no predetermined path or destination, no particular aim in mind, save the discovery of reality," according to R. Lane Kauffmann in his essay on the essayist's methods. Most essayists, then, in their search for form, use what Walter Pater called an "un-methodical method."

Finally, there is a sharp contrast between the world where excavations take place and the world one finds when she reemerges. "Once well underground," reports the Mole in *The Wind and the Willows*, "you know exactly where you are. Nothing can happen to you, and nothing can get at you. You're entirely your own master, and you don't have to consult anybody or mind what they say. Things go on all the same overhead and you let 'em, and don't bother about 'em. When you want to, up you go, and there the things are, waiting for you." Predators, weather, shadows, nesting materials, and nosy mammalogists. The essayist opens the door of her study to find hungry children, dirty laundry, a ringing telephone, and an empty bank account.

Nature's other gifts present a single focus or one focus sharper and more engaging than the rest as soon as I perceived them. The mole, however, is too full of essay-worthy possibilities. More coats than pegs to hang them on. Too many directions in which I could dig my path. So many slants, I can't handle my subject. Too many tricks in this bag. With a little more time, a little more paper, and someone to tend the children just a little longer, I'd have a dozen more angles. But enough is enough. All these speculations have brought me no nearer to an essay about the mole than when I began.

"I do not see the whole of anything," Michel de Montaigne assures me. "Of a hundred members and faces that each thing has, I take one, sometimes only to pick it, sometimes to brush the surface, sometimes to pinch it to the bone." For Montaigne, it was a matter of picking a course and following it, accepting that some paths must remain untraveled, some members and faces undeveloped. So, too, for me. If I've come this far, I have selected a path and pursued it. But whose furry surface have I brushed? What creature have I tried to pinch to the bone?

I examine my own meanderings. I walk beside raised ridges. I remember how my excavations connect one mountain to the next. From this distance I see that what appeared to be an essay about the mole in reality was—from the papillae on each tentacle to the tip of the sleek tail to each clod of earth moved—an essay about essaying.

Winter 1993

# SKY WATCH

*I*t is thirty-six degrees at 8 P.M., three days before Thanksgiving, and the sky above Lincoln, Nebraska, is clear. My binoculars are pointed to the heavens, as they have been most evenings during the past two weeks. Since white light makes the eyes less sensitive, my flashlight is covered with red paper. I study the diagram of the autumn sky in *Olcott's Field Book of the Stars*. I hope to find Cepheus's leaning house, Cassiopeia's crown, Orion's hourglass, but I am not successful.

The night sky is a huge and moving connect-the-dot picture. Isaac Asimov says that on an average clear night, two thousand points of light are visible to the naked eye. I suppose there are hundreds of thousands of ways to connect these dots, yet I do not try. How much I have changed since first grade, when I happily ignored the numbered dots and found my own forms. But now my single-minded goal is to impose the field book map onto the celestial sphere, to see what others have seen, to find what is constant.

Part of the problem is that the names for the heavenly forms that I have inherited are Mediterranean, but I am not. If I could conceive of the star groupings as a cottonwood seedhead, a sandhill crane, a Mormon Trail handcart, or Crazy Horse, I'd be on firmer ground. But the heavens are Greek to me, and one book sends me to another. Consider Andromeda, the name of a well-known constellation, a name suggesting maleness to me (from the Greek *andros*, man). I consult several mythologies and learn that Andromeda's mother, Queen Cassiopeia, enraged the sea nymphs when she claimed that her daughter was more beautiful than they. The sea nymphs told their father, Neptune, about the insult, and he in turn punished Cassiopeia's vanity by sending Cetus, the sea monster, to ravage the Ethiopian coast. Andromeda's parents were so alarmed by the devastation that her father, Cepheus, consulted the Oracle, who advised that only one act could appease the gods and so save the kingdom: chaining Andromeda to a rock and allowing the leviathan to prey upon her. Heartbroken, Cepheus obeyed. Just as the sea monster was about to kill Andromeda, Perseus, fresh from his victorious battle with the Gorgon, flashed the head of the Medusa before the sea monster, who gazed upon it and was turned to stone. Perseus cut Andromeda's chains and bore her away on his steed, Pegasus. Andromeda and her seacoast were saved.

Accounts of the myth are similar, but the ways in which the chained goddess is given form in the heavens are not. Patrick Moore draws one almost straight line from the top right corner of the square of Pegasus and two lines shooting from the end of that line for his Andromeda. William T. Olcott connects the dots in such a way that two rays or legs shoot from the same corner of Pegasus. Kelvin McKready draws Andromeda like a broken television antenna: a bent base, one of the two tee-crosses half missing. Not one of these drawings has any connection to the myth that I can see (are the two lines Andromeda's arms? her legs? Andromeda and Cetus? Andromeda and Perseus? the chains without the woman?). Nor can I locate this constellation in the heavens. My foray into mythology has not revealed a single mystery of the universe.

My grandmother, a modern-day primitive, planted potatoes, cut her hair, and potty-trained her children according to the phase of the moon, but I cannot say where the moon is in its monthly journey around the sun or where it hangs in the autumn or summer sky. Nor do I share my ancestors' gratitude for the full moon's brightness or their dread of a new moon's darkness. I don't know which stars can lead me home. I can't tell the time of the night by the relation of Cassiopeia's squat W to Polaris. I know my sign of the zodiac and sometimes read my daily horoscope in the newspaper, but I can't locate Virgo in the sky. If I glimpse a solar or lunar eclipse it is only because it was forecast on the television news and I was urged outside to observe. Last chance for three years. Yet, I am searching for order and certainty not where I am likely to find it (bird migrations or the progression of flowing creek to beaver-dammed pond to solid ground) but in that unknowable place the ancients called Chaos.

Within Andromeda is a misty cloud, the Great Spiral. This smudge of stars is the galaxy nearest our own, yet it is so far away it takes 2.3 million years for its light to reach earth. Since Andromeda is 200,000 light-years across and contains 300,000,000,000 stars, it is larger than our own galaxy—or at least it once was. "When we look out into space," says Patrick Moore, "we also look backward in time; we are seeing the Spiral not as it is now, but as it used to be two million years ago." I can barely conceive of time beyond the short space of my lifetime. The largest space I can conceive of is the distance between Nebraska and Vermont, which I traveled by car with two bored children and a cranky husband. It seemed an eternity. Asimov says that astronomers suspect the total number of galaxies in the parts of the universe we can observe with our best instruments to be as high as 100,000,000,000, though with a little more looking, the number could climb. I am not ready to believe such facts about time and space as Moore and Asimov present. I must first experience my own Copernican Revolution.

Many ancient people conceived of the earth as a large flat disk floating in the center surface of a world ocean, with the stars and planets affixed to a great hollow shell rotating overhead. Aristotle and his Greek contemporaries not only believed that the heavens were fixed, but they also thought that the heavenly bodies were made of a superior substance free from all change. Quite logically, people assigned their deities to this immutable, unreachable place. Eliphaz asked Job: "Is not God in the height of heaven? and behold the height of the stars, how high they are!" In times of trouble, the psalmist lifted his eyes to the hills for help, but when things were bleakest, he looked beyond to the heavens.

In Europe during the Middle Ages, the popular and Church-approved conception of creation presented the universe in layers. In the center of the cosmos was the earth. Closest to earth was the heaven of the moon, followed by the heavens of the planets, the heavens of the fixed stars, the crystalline heaven, and, finally, the Lord's heaven, the seat of God, the saints, and the saved. This picture matches my experience of the world more closely than does anything astronomers tell me. "Our eyes bear witness to the revolution of the heavens," Martin Luther observed. To say the sun sets and the moon rises is to speak the truth. Except in small surface matters—the slow erosion of rock, strip mining, the sudden movement of fault planes, the belch of lava—the earth *is* immovable. The stars and planets that twinkle and orbit in the outer reaches of darkness are mere background.

But not mere background. I read that the average distance between stars is three parsecs (ten light-years or about 60,000,000,000,000 miles). First I visualized this distance as one-dimensional, occurring horizontally or vertically. After all, the heavens are a firmament, the solid vault of the sky. But I lost my biblical perspective when I realized I had to focus my binoculars when shifting from one star to the next just as I did when watching birds. Not all birds are the same distance from me; neither are all stars. The sky is not a flat felt board to which cutout stars cling. I suspect that when Galileo looked through his homemade spyglass for the first time, he was taken aback not only by the sheer number of new stars, the satellites orbiting Jupiter, mountains on the moon, or spots on the sun, but also by the new depth of space.

Copernicus was not the first to postulate a sun-centered universe. The rishis of ancient India wrote of heliocentric motion as well as the earth's daily axial revolution, the law of gravitation, the presence of fixed stars, and the reflected light of the moon 4,500 years before Copernicus's birth. Apparently the ancient Maya also grasped the way the universe works, since their advanced astronomical-calendrical calculations began in 3113 B.C. Aristarchus of Samos insisted that the earth moves around the sun in the third century B.C., but his contemporaries would not budge from their position at the center of Ptolemy's universe. In Copernicus's own century, the German cardinal Nicholas Krebs suggested that the earth was not the stationary center of the cosmos, but his impiety was also ignored.

Ptolemy relied on eccentrics (orbits whose centers do not coincide with the center, which is the earth, in this case) and epicycles (orbits around the center of a circle that in turn is orbiting the center of a larger circle) to account for the seemingly irregular movements of the planets around the earth. In his search for a simpler, less complicated explanation, Copernicus measured the movements of the planets, which led him to the heretical conclusion that the earth and the other planets moved around the sun. But Copernicus was a man of his times: he maintained that the planets moved in perfect circles, since nothing less than perfection could be assigned to the heavens. In truth, the orbits are elliptical. Consequently, Copernicus also relied on complicated epicycles to account for the apparent movement of the outer planets. Mars, for instance, appears to draw a backward S as it orbits the sun. First it moves counterclockwise through the stars. Next it appears to stand still for a few days, since it moves in a slower, larger orbit than the earth. Then it appears to move backward. Finally, it proceeds counterclockwise.

By 1533 Copernicus had worked out his entire theory, but he knew there would be nothing but trouble with the Church if he published it. To calm the waters, he dedicated *De Revolutionibus Orbium Coelestium* (Concerning the Revolutions of the Celestial Bodies) to Pope Paul III. Osiander, Copernicus's publisher, further quelled the waves by penning an anonymous preface to the volume stating that heliocentrism was a hypothesis, a teaching tool, a theoretical premise through which astronomers could make their celestial observations understandable to their students. It did not, however, reflect reality or probability. Some readers believed the qualification was Copernicus's own. As legend tells it, the great stargazer's timing was impeccable: the first printed copy of his theory reached him in 1543, just hours before he died. (Some say he would have lived longer had he not seen Osiander's preface.) Nonetheless, Copernicus was spared knowing that for many decades, his book of revolutions would be all but forgotten.

Old theories die slowly, especially when they more greatly elevate human significance than the new ones. Bertrand Russell says that Copernicus's theory intended "the dethronement of our planet from its central position," which "suggests to the imagination a similar dethronement of its inhabitants." If earth is no more significant than the sun and stars and planets, then perhaps we are not the crown and purpose of creation as once supposed. In the early 1600s, insisting that the earth moved was such an iconoclastic statement that men who uttered it were silenced or martyred. It wasn't until 1687, when Isaac Newton showed that gravitation accounted for the motions of comets, planets, and the moon, that the scale was tipped in favor of heliocentrism. Still, *De Revolutionibus* and those works that defended Copernicus's theory were not removed from the Church's index of prohibited books until 1835. Still, such distinguished universities as Harvard and Yale continued to teach the Ptolemaic and Copernican systems side by side.

None of the standard biographical information about Copernicus and his age reveals what I really want to know: how he *felt* when he realized there were seven planets instead of six, the newest addition being Earth; how he felt when he realized that the only foundation he would ever know was not the stable center. Did such revelations lead Copernicus—perhaps a devout man, perhaps an atheist, but shaped by Church teachings nonetheless—to muse with the psalmist: "When I consider the heavens, the work of thy fingers, the moon and the stars, which thou hast ordained; What is man, that thou art mindful of him?" Nearly five centuries after Copernicus died, Harlow Shapley further reduced our stature by asserting that the actual center of our lens-shaped galaxy is not the sun, but twenty-five thousand light-years away in Sagittarius: there lies the galactic center around which it takes our sun two hundred million years to rotate. As if the blow dealt to human prestige by the nineteenth-century geologists was not devastating enough when they informed us that configurations in the earth's crust had required no mere six thousand years as suggested by the Hebrew scriptures but entire millennia, we now learn that we are a speck near the rim, far from our galactic hub, which is itself just one of a billion or more galaxies.

On Thanksgiving Eve I entertain myself with a star that appears large and single to the naked eye but cleaves before my binoculars. Back and forth I go. I wonder if I am seeing optical doubles (stars that line up together but are really far apart) or binary stars (true stellar companions revolving around a common center). Then, through the binoculars, a streak. I do not know what I have seen form and disappear in an instant. I do not know what disaster this streak portends. I cap my binoculars and put them in the case.

Five years on the Great Plains has accustomed me to big skies, yet nothing could prepare me for the cosmic perspective that stargazing provides. It's cold out there in outer space and growing colder. Space is expanding so that we can't even contemplate an edge to the universe. Clusters of galaxies drift farther and farther apart, beyond the edge of our observable universe. My awareness expands to fill intergalactic space the way the smallest job can expand to fill an entire workday. I imagine the Deists' god, watching the cosmic machine run. To him, a series of wars, a long, virulent epidemic, and another ice age or two on the fourth planet from the sun near the edge of the Milky Way are but star dust. If the earth blows up, it is of less consequence than my hitting the delete button and erasing one of the two hundred thousand words stored in my computer. Gone without a trace. Of so much less consequence is my stormy marriage, my father's weak heart, my daily failings, and all the other things I pray about.

My awareness contracts slowly, like the mass of a new star. It is yet too intergalactic to be contained in a small, warm place lit by electric lights. It is not yet contracted enough for me to deem typing sky notes onto a tiny computer screen as a labor whose fruits matter in the grand scheme of things. I stroll around my yard kicking leaves. I examine the frozen, stalky remains of last summer's vegetable garden. When the Lakota ghost dancers returned to the earth and their bodies after journeying to the Spiritland, they found star flesh and moon rocks clenched in their fists. I return from my journey through the stars with only frozen fingers and toes, a neck stiff from being too long bent back, and a deepened sense of my own insignificance before the cold, black expanse.

I settle in bed with several astronomy books, hoping that facts and big numbers will lull me to sleep. I read that the sun is a ball of hot gases kept together by the force of gravity. If the gravitational field of the sun increases, we will be pulled into its boiling cauldron and cooked like lobsters. If gravity lessens, we will drift toward the moving edge of the universe like pieces of spacecraft junk. Even if the gravitational field holds, we are more likely to die by fire than by ice. Hans Bethe calculated that the sun is becoming hotter and more luminous as it consumes more fuel, losing mass at the rate of four million tons per second. It is just a matter of time before the sun ignites the earth. In 1717, Edmond Halley demonstrated that our solar system is not anchored securely at a fixed spot in space but is sailing in a great star-swirl toward an undetermined location, with no pilots or flight controllers in sight. Likewise Andromeda, our closest galactic neighbor, is making a beeline toward us. Asimov says the earth spins in wide circles, like a dying top. The uncertainty of this image chills me. If we stop spinning, half our planet will be perpetually bright and burning, the other half perpetually dark and cold, the latter an ideal place for around-the-clock stargazing. Ironically, if Earth did not orbit the sun, if the sun did not orbit the galactic center, if the whole show were not drifting, we would lose our stability. I hold my breath. The machine must keep running. This year, my Thanksgiving prayer has a cosmic scope.

But my prayer brings me no peace. What hubris is this to believe that my petitions could reach God's heaven, beyond the farthest star? I dream the familiar nightmare that I am falling, falling, but instead of from a cliff, I am hurtling through deepest space, where nothing breaks my fall. If there is life on other planets, it does not appear in any form I can recognize. My real horror comes not from the unending descent but from my realization that I am utterly, eternally alone.

In the light of day, my fears recede. Venus, morning star, hangs in pink layered clouds between the blinking red lights of a radio tower and the ominous outline of a cellular telephone transmitter. The heavens are solid and near.

When I was twenty and too self-absorbed to appreciate most of what happened to me, a friend and I kept a couple of astronomy students company while they kept night watch at the observatory. Most of what I saw through the huge tele-scope seemed unfocused, contextless. But I did learn the distinctive form of the Pleiades: it is the one constellation I can always find.

In mythology, Pleiades are the pillars that support the heavens—a job that modern astronomy reveals is much more impressive than that of Atlas, the father of the Seven Sisters, who merely bore the weight of the world on his shoulders. Legend tells that only six stars are visible; the invisible seventh is the "Lost Pleiade." However, more than seven stars are visible in this cluster. In 1580, thirty years before Galileo reinvented the telescope, Michael Maest-lin—who must have had exceptionally keen vision and lived beneath excep-tionally clear skies—plotted eleven stars. Galileo saw only six with his naked eye; through his spyglass he counted thirty-six. Asimov reports that nine stars can be made out with the naked eye, though some are too close to separate. A professional telescope can reveal 250 of the probable 750 stars in the cluster. I am frustrated that so much is beyond the range of my binoculars.

Pleiades is a tight little cluster of stars moving together at the same velocity, in the same direction. Like a flock of birds, Olcott says. The spaces between them are only one-third that of the average distance between stars in my neigh-borhood, yet Pleiades occupies a vast area: seventy light-years in diameter. James Hickey says that two stars in Pleiades might be farther apart than the sun and distant Vega in Lyre, though they are still members of the same clus-ter. And where is this twinkling stellar flock heading? It is converging on a definite location in the heavens, about five degrees east of Betelgeuse, the red-dish supergiant that forms Orion's right shoulder.

It might appear that when God asked Job, "Canst thou bind the sweet influence of Pleiades, or loose the bands of Orion?" the deity's intent was to prove its own power and Job's comparative powerlessness, but I believe God was planting a seed, intimating things to come. With a little more knowledge of the way things worked, Job could have answered yes to God's question. Ten centuries later, Jesus would speak of a universe of contingencies: whatever is bound on earth shall be bound in heaven; whatever is loosed on earth shall be loosed in heaven. Nineteen centuries later, physicists would also speak of a universe of contingencies: our universe ripples with invisible fields that ex-ist throughout time and space, as opposed to a particle that exists at only one point in time. My dictionary of physics says that field theory was intro-duced to explain the interaction of particles or bodies through space. An elec-tric charge, for instance, modifies the space around it so that another charge in this region experiences a force. That region is an electric field. Tweak one end of a field and a wiggle moves through it. The tweak is felt over there and over there and over there. What you loose on earth is loosed in heaven. Some scientists postulate that consciousness, too, is a field and that each thought is a tweak that ripples through the entire field. Whatever you loose on earth— from the vaguest impulse in the human mind to a nuclear explosion—*is* loosed in heaven. Thus, if I can find Pleiades from my spot on earth, I can bind her in heaven. If I can bind Pleiades, I can loosen Orion's belt, unchain Andromeda's arms, set Pegasus upright, and break Polaris's grip on Little Bear's tail. Pleiades is the center upon which my heavens hinge.

After one night of thick clouds and two nights of snowfall, I am in my front yard again, gazing at the heavens. It is ten degrees, hard, cold, and clear at forty degrees north latitude, ninety-five degrees west longitude.

I locate Pleiades in the heavens. I locate Pleiades in McKready's 1912 star book, which presents two maps of the December first sky at 8 P.M. in my part of the world: "before" (no superimposed patterns) and "after" (lines drawn between the dots). By working with both illustrations, I move directly up from Pleiades and find the curve of Perseus's breast, the reach of his sword. I drop my head back further and I am before Cassiopeia's throne, which tonight looks like an M set on end. Mysteries fall like dominoes. Andromeda clings to wild Pegasus. Cepheus peaks. Draco coils around Little Bear. Hercules kneels.

I pay no mind to the snow I've been standing in for half an hour or to my terror of falling into the fathomless void. I go to the backyard, where the Big Dipper is my only point of reference. I am never as certain about this constellation as I am about Pleiades. First, I find the bright polestar. The bowl of the Dipper is directly beneath it. I descend until I fall in line with the two heads and four feet of Gemini. Then I perch a moment on variable Betelgeuse, slide down a band of three stars, and rest on blue-white Rigel: Orion, the hunter with his bow taut.

Sir James Jeans observed that the stars are not "a mere random collection of points of light . . . [but] the same ordered arrangement persist[s] night after night." A 1912 star map of the skies above Nebraska is accurate eighty-three years later. I cannot say the same about an eighty-three-year-old map of the terra firma. Yet, eighty-three years is but a blink when measured against sidereal time. Once the polestar was Thuban in Draco; presently it is Polaris in Ursa Minor; by A.D. 14,000 it will be bright Vega in Lyra. Ptolemy did not catalog Alcyone in A.D. 145, yet now it is the brightest star in Pleiades. Two stars in the Big Dipper—one at the tip of the handle, the other at the outer rim of the bowl—are moving away from the other five. By the year 200,000, the constellation will bear no resemblance to a ladle. Like us, stars are born and move and die. Eighty-three years of sameness proves nothing.

Our universe is a moving thing, oscillating, expanding, collapsing, compressing, and expanding again. Just one big bang, just one black hole after another. All flesh is grass and so is all that I leave for posterity—children, essays, a few kind deeds. Heaven and earth will pass away, but before they do, time will loosen Orion's belt and broaden his shoulders. In fifty-five thousand years, he will be a shorter, stouter man. McKready observes that the mythology of the constellation we now call Orion has taken so many forms that it is impossible to say which should have precedence in age or interest. Yet people have remained constant in the earthly form with which they have identified this particular cluster: it is a hunter. I see the same forms as did my Paleolithic ancestors who ordered their lives by the phases of the moon and the migrations of the stars. Constancy lies not in the heavens but in the patterns projected onto the heavens from earth. That is as much constancy as I can hope for in a spinning, drifting, dying, and re-creating cosmos.

November 1993

# HARD REMAINS

The moment the deep, hollow shell met the palm of my hand and my fingers closed around it, I was no longer waiting at the Encounter Center at the Children's Zoo while my son examined a live boa, nor was it the last day of September. Instead, I was a child in my great-grandfather "Pop's" bedroom, a sunless place that reeked of Beechnut tobacco and years of infirmity. I do not recall if he was there or not, but my great-aunt Pertsie was. She was preparing to lift down and show me something from the top of a chest of drawers that I was too short to see. Then, it was there: the upper half of a turtle shell upturned and pedestaled atop a short rod firmly footed in a round piece of wood. The shell did not rest level like a bathtub, but aslant, tail end up. Within glittered my great-aunt's rhinestone brooches, her beaded clip-on earrings, and the rings from her first two marriages. I rested the laden shell in the palm of my hand, the cool metal rod parting my second and third fingers.

Many years ago, my great-aunt explained, her youngest brother and my favorite great-uncle crafted this jewel bowl for her. Supposedly, he found the turtle on one of his trucking runs from Oklahoma City to Los Angeles, a run that for decades provided blessed relief from his tongues-speaking wife, Maxine, and that also provided tales of his highway exploits too tall to believe. Once back in Oklahoma, Great-uncle Buster parted the upper and lower shells, scraped them clean, cooked and ate the flesh, mounted the domed upper shell, and then sent it to his sister in Iowa.

My great-aunt tenderly lifted the bowl from my hands and removed it from my sight. Once again, it was the last day of September and I was waiting at the Encounter Center, cradling a comparatively weightless turtle shell in my left palm, wondering about origins and returns.

My turtle shell memory troubles me. For one thing, I've yet to find anyone who can verify the existence of this remembered artifact. My great-aunt is dead, and so are her husband and two ex-husbands. My mother and grandmother cannot recollect the shell. My brothers are younger than I, spent less time in that old house than I, and consequently remember less about it. The only likely source of verification lies with Great-uncle Buster. But as seldom as I communicate with him—lately, only at family funerals—I would feel foolish writing to inquire the whereabouts of a possibly fictitious reptile shell.

Other problems exist. I sometimes wonder if I didn't confuse this turtle shell with a conch that my grandparents acquired during their "Texas Era," an eight-year period when they and my mother lived in various Gulf Coast cities while my grandfather built bridges and factories, a period that despite its brevity has since acquired mythic proportions, a period against which most other events of their lives are held in relation ("It must have been four years after we returned from Texas" or "These barbecued ribs are good, but they're nothing like the ones we had in Pasadena").

This Texas conch is buff-white, peaked and turreted on the outside, glossy and tropical pink within. The outer lip curls back and under, exposing an inner lip stitched with dark brown. The conch sits aslant on a round wooden stand, but "Galveston, Texas," printed in black cursive on the exterior of the shell, is parallel to the surface on which it sits. This shell is illuminated by a small white bulb within; an electrical cord extends out the back. The similarities between it and the turtle shell jewel bowl are obvious: both are mounted on stands; both sit aslant; both are exoskeletons of soft-bodied creatures; both are remnants of a legendary past made functional in the present.

Another problem worries me. I do not know to what extent my turtle shell memory has been reconstructed by the chronic revisionist in me. Some details are true but embellished. Others are fictions, I admit. Yet other details are borrowed from other people's accounts of related experiences. Recently, when I asked my mother if she recalled the turtle shell jewel bowl ("What shell?" she asked), she in turn asked if I remembered the smell of Pop's tobacco. I did not, nor could I recall him chewing and spitting. Yet this detail is now so much a part of my memory that, yes, I do remember the smell of Pop's Beechnut chewing tobacco.

Now I find that I have told my revised and embellished account so many times that I can no longer separate the facts from the fictions. The same was true of my grandfather, a more chronic revisionist and embellisher than I. He bored and delighted his listeners with extravagant tales about his travels and exploits as a member of the world's greatest brotherhood, ironworkers. Even though his stories were highly improbable, none of us communicated our disbelief. Except once. On this particular occasion, the story hinged upon a cocky foreman who couldn't read blueprints. Danger was imminent. The location: San Francisco's Golden Gate Bridge. The story was progressing at a fair clip when my grandmother interrupted. "When did you ever work on the Golden Gate Bridge?"

"1935," my grandfather answered gruffly.

"No, you didn't. That was the year Daughter was born. You were right here in Keokuk with us. You've never even been to California. Especially in 1935."

My grandfather paused only a moment before rescuing the foreman suspended thousands of feet above the Bay. Nor was this the last time I heard the tale. In fact, my grandfather told this story so often and so convincingly, I believe that when he evoked his peak experiences for one final viewing, he was standing atop a 4,200-foot-long suspension bridge. Say the story often enough and it is your reality.

I admit I never saw wedding rings in the turtle shell, though I said I did. Until her death, my great-aunt not only wore the rings from her third husband, Harvey, but from her second husband, Bud, as well. I know nothing of the rings from her first, brief marriage to the Greek. This means that the rings from her first two marriages were not in the shell as I said they were. Nor do I honestly recollect a "cool metal rod parting my second and third fingers." It is an imagined but plausible sensation. I can just as easily picture the shell sitting flush against the wooden stand, in which case I could not have held the shell as I said I did.

Perhaps anything handed down from high, unseen regions is memorable. So, too, the macabre, and the transformation of a dead body part to some practical or decorative use certainly qualifies as such. Moreover, anything and anyone associated with that old log house my great-grandfather built near the confluence of the Mississippi and Des Moines Rivers is a priceless relic of a mythical past that I cannot bear to lose. Even though there are other places where I spent more time and of which I possess more lucid memories, it is that log house that provides the most recurrent setting for my dreams. It is a place weighted with value. It is a laden ship sunk to the bottom, immovable, preserved in the cool tranquillity of deep waters. It is the mathematical basin of attraction to which my calculations keep returning. It is the gravitational field of a great star that keeps dragging its own light back to itself, never permitting escape. It is the place to which I return again and again.

Along Route 66 where my great-aunt claimed her jewel bowl had its origins, one might encounter—at least among the turtle species I know—a painted, a western box, a yellow, a softshell, a snapper, or a gopher. Yet when I imagine the live donor, I do not see it lumbering along the edge of a southwestern highway but bubbling in muddy river waters, perhaps in the Des Moines, the Skunk, or the Mississippi. Around those waters, turtles are abundant—blandings, Mississippi painteds, midland sawbacks, snappers, eastern boxes, muds, and musks (the last two I exclude as possibilities, since most people find them inedible). But it is on one of the most common turtles that I'd place my money. The elegant slider is abundant, edible, and at once plain and fancy. Its upper shell is smooth, flat, and dark khaki in color, but the rear is roughly serrated, a decorative conclusion to an otherwise modest affair.

While I can only guess the species and origins of my great-aunt's turtle shell jewel bowl, scientists speak with some certainty about its evolutionary origins. Paleontologists believe that the evolutionary link between the ancient cotylosaur, the stem reptile from which all reptiles originated, and the present-day turtle may be *Eunotosaurus africanus*. The 250-million-year-old bones of this turtleish creature are so poorly preserved that scientists cannot determine if *Eunotosaurus*'s skull lacks openings for the ear, as do the skulls of present-day turtles, and there is no trace of a lower shell. Yet, *Eunotosaurus*'s hard remains reveal eight ribs—the beginnings of a shell.

The shell of the modern turtle has remained unchanged for the better part of the past 175 million years. The carapace, or upper shell, is an exoskeleton, a combination of ribs and bony plates also worn by crabs and armadillos but by no other reptiles. It is, in fact, about fifty bones fused together. Horny shields or plates composed of keratin, the same fibrous protein from which our nails and hair are made, form the outer covering of the shell. These "laminae" are an integral part of the carapace in some species, but in others they are periodically shed and replaced. It is the laminae—their coloring, their reticulations, in some cases, their complete absence—that permit swiftest identification of most species: the wood turtle, so sculpted that it appears to be transporting a hillful of grooved pyramids; the undivided, leathery covering of the softshell turtle, which has entirely replaced the hard laminae.

I knew nothing of the turtle's evolution on that day at the zoo when I cradled the hollow carapace in the palm of my hand. Once I returned from my plunge into my past, I saw the short rafters shooting laterally from the spine at the apex of the shell, and I wondered about them. Enough so that I carried thick manuals of chelonian structure and physiology home from the life sciences library. Several days in a row, I visited skeletal tortoise remains at the natural history museum. I browsed through local pet shops until I purchased "Argo," an eastern box turtle, as much a gift for myself as for my son's sixth birthday. And during those few weeks, I slid effortlessly back and forth through evolutionary time.

Turtle bones are like human bones in the most elemental sense. Both are made of calcium phosphate, the chemical compound responsible for the bone's hardness. Remove the calcium phosphate and the bones become flexible—enough so that one can literally tie them in knots. It is the calcium phosphate that permits the bones to endure for a lifetime or for entire geologic periods like those of *Eunotosaurus africanus*. These bones, or rather the deposits of calcium phosphate in these bones, are the hard remains. For those who leave behind no records of their thoughts or deeds, these bones are all that remain. Once our livingness is gone, once that fleeting moment is gone in which our livingness is remembered by children, grandchildren, and sometimes great-grandchildren, our biography is borne by our bones.

Our bones reveal our genetic inheritances, environmental choices, and necessities. Loren Eiseley, perhaps our most articulate and contemplative bone-hunter, demonstrates just how detailed osteo-biography can be. As an anthropologist, his task was to reclothe old bones with personality, to help the bones tell their own stories. And that he did. One skeleton brought to him was that of a young woman who had fallen or been struck, resulting in a dangerous compound fracture, a wound that today would mandate months of hospitalization. Though the injury left her permanently disfigured—the orbit of her left eye dropped a quarter of an inch—she recovered, which was especially remarkable given her circumstances: no medical attention and the endless travels of a hunting society. Even though the woman's doom was "not written in the bones," Eiseley speculated that it, too, was by violent means, since her skull was drawn not from a grave but from beneath the waters of a giant river.

Once flesh and breath are gone, we are but calcium sticks, as Eiseley observes. And those hard remains may be as close to immortality as we will ever come.

Injunctions against the desecration of bones are universal. Sir James Frazer reports that members of hunting societies believe that the bones of their dead prey communicate with their living animal kin. If treated with respect, the dead beckon the living; if treated with disrespect—being tossed to the dogs or thrown in the fire, for instance—they warn their kin away. In the Timor Islands, fishermen once hung skulls of all the turtles they had caught under their houses. Before going forth to catch another, they spoke to the skull of their last quarry, beseeching its spirit to enter its living kin so they, too, could be taken. Vestiges of this belief persist, especially in the form of prohibitions against the burning of bones. In *Fisher Folk-lore* (1965), Peter Frederick Anson confesses that he so absorbed the fisher taboos and superstitions from the northeastern coast of Scotland that even at the age of seventy-five "nothing would induce me to throw fish bones on the fire."

It is not just the integrity of animal bones that we are charged to preserve. When the ancient Greeks sacrificed to their gods, it wasn't the flesh or the hide or the heart they offered but the bones wrapped in fat. The Jews were cautioned not to break a single bone of the Passover lamb, an injunction that was still observed at the crucifixion. Joseph instructed the Israelites, "God will visit you, and you shall carry up my bones from here." Moses fulfilled that command when he led his people out of Egypt.

I know of a small cemetery—just a few cedar trees and five or six dozen untended graves—surrounded by prime commercially zoned land. To the north, a car dealership. To the south, a shopping mall. To the east, an apartment complex. To the west, a department store. But simply because this plot bears bones, its future is secure. It is as though each headstone repeats the words on Shakespeare's tomb: "Bleste be ye man yt spares thes stones. And cvrst be he yt moves my bones." No one will ever sell hamburgers on that plot of land.

These injunctions exist for good reason. Frazer says that the members of hunting societies believed that in time, the well-preserved bones of their dead prey would be reclothed with flesh and quickened with life. The Lapps buried bones believing that the animals would be restored in another world. Some Native Americans, however, believed that reanimation took place here and now. Thus, on the Great Plains, circles and symmetrical piles of buffalo skulls once awaited regeneration.

Ezekiel, with a little divine assistance, restored flesh and breathed new life into the Valley of Dry Bones, "and they lived, and stood upon their feet, an exceedingly great host." The seeds of life, the "bone soul" if you will, resides in the hard remains, and there begins resurrection.

I collect the seeds of creation. The forespaces of my bookshelves are so lined with hard remains—snail shells, clams, a turreted seashell, crinoids, coral, part of a deer pelvis, the femur of a mammal I've yet to identify—that my books are beyond my reach. Presently, I am waiting while the soft parts of a dead pigeon decay near the railroad tracks. Once the bones are clean, I'll make room for them too. At night, I dream a landscape strewn with thimble-size mouse skulls. I walk in an old part of town because mounted to the side of an old shed at the end of a graveled alley are two skulls: one large, a cow perhaps; the other, smaller, a large dog or a pronghorn, I guess. I covet these. Enough so that to possess beautifully weathered skulls with parts jaggedly missing or skulls so fresh that swatches of hide and hair still remain could cause me to clear my shelves of books once and for all and to read bones instead. Then, many times a day, I'd pause before rows of jawbones and crania, frightening yet consoling symbols of mortality and permanence.

The mind also bears hard remains—images or splinters of images clearly retained and hard forgotten. But memory is inscrutable. What it chooses to remember is as curious as what it chooses to forget. I do not, for instance, remember my first day of school, yet I do remember coming home from school those first few weeks, standing atop a crumbling wall, the same wall from which I once extracted crinoids like loose baby teeth, and dropping pop bottles one by one onto the brick alley below, watching them shatter. And while most of my birthdays are hazy, I remember with stunning clarity the first one I spent alone (I was twenty), in bed early on a Saturday night reading E. L. Doctorow after a dinner of eggs and toast.

We seek secure homes for these hard remains, too—high, sturdy shelves where they will not be lost or broken. I have observed those who knew in their bones that their time was near and that safe storage had to be found for the ossified remains of their experiences. I was with my Great-aunt Pertsie when she learned of the teacup-size tumors in her lymph glands. I wanted to talk of specialists, tests, alternative treatments, and drugs that would help her sleep. But she wanted to speak of more pressing concerns than the small, mechanical details about how her life would end. On the day of her diagnosis, she told me about Carrie Nation, who eighty-seven years earlier to the day, busted up the Wichita saloon. The same Carrie Nation whose framed portrait Pop hung in his bedroom. The same Carrie Nation whose husband, David, married my great-grandparents someplace in Oklahoma. The bride had worn a red blouse, a blue skirt, and had ridden sidesaddle to the ceremony. My great-aunt also spoke of the willow grove near Montrose, Iowa, where she and Pop gathered boughs to sell to the Keokuk broom factory. She spoke of her mother's gall-bladder attack (first, they thought it was her heart) and how it came while she was frying off the last of the hog Pop had butchered. Before leaving for the hospital, my great-grandmother had instructed her daughters to finish the job, but as soon as she was out of sight, Pertsie and my grandmother chunked the rest of the meat down the toilet hole. My great-aunt spoke of Nettie and her husband, who had lived in a tent in Pop's front yard for nearly two years while Nettie's husband built the Mississippi River bridge. And my great-aunt spoke of taking turns with her brothers grinding horseradish downwind from the house, crying as they worked.

I have never discovered willow groves near Montrose, a framed photograph of Carrie Nation, a broom factory in Keokuk, nor can I imagine spending two Iowa winters in a tent no matter how efficient the stove. Yet these are the remains my great-aunt chose to leave. As long as I keep them, her past is alive.

Sometimes hard remains are offered with a playful, hopeful tone; other times in the insistent, pleading manner of those who know that time is short and a willing repository has yet to be found. I heard urgent pleas at the nursing home where I once worked as a cook, where some residents spilled their memories to any passing shadow. I have heard urgent pleas from the old, hump-backed bachelor across the alley who stops me each time I pass. I have heard urgent pleas from my neighbor Marie, who enticed my son into her house with chocolate cookies and new toys so she could tell me about her eighty-three years in Lincoln's Russian Bottoms. On several occasions she showed me a smooth, buff-colored stone with a bur on the end. It was her husband's, Lloyd's, kidney stone, removed a few days before he died—the biggest stone the surgeon had ever seen. "I'm going to get it listed in that *Guinness Book of World Records*," Marie assured me. It was the safest place she could find for that hard remain.

These storytellers ask me to accept their memories, to hold them dear, to make them part of myself. But if I were to accept all of them, in time I would resemble a carrier snail, which cements rocks and dead shells to her back with her own secretions until eventually she is a creeping pile of debris.

Accepting another's hard remains does not mean that I accept those memories as truthful accounts. In our retellings of the past, we seek atonement, fulfill our yearnings, and guardedly reveal our inner selves. Consequently, most excursions into the past are more attempts to right the record than credible eyewitness accounts.

Consider, for instance, what I have learned of my great-great-uncle Abner Bunker of Montrose, as renowned for his fiddling finesse at barn dances as for his failure to feed his wife and five children. One day while Ab was strolling down Elm Street toward the Mississippi, a child on either side of him, a townsman approached and shot him dead. My grandmother insisted that Ab had been stealing milk from the farmer's cow for too long. My great-aunt Pertsie maintained that Ab had been fiddling with the farmer's wife. I have found nothing to confirm or deny either story. In fact, I have found no evidence of Ab Bunker's existence in either the state historical society archives or the Montrose cemetery. I doubt the veracity of both my great-aunt's and my grandmother's accounts. Yet I know that even if hard evidence were produced that refuted one or both of their theories about the murder—the farmer's deposition or an incriminating page from a diary, perhaps—each storyteller would staunchly uphold her version.

Research on memory suggests that the tendency to believe one's own story in the face of refuting evidence is universal. In his 1956 study "Learning and Retaining Verbal Material," Harry Kay demonstrated that when test subjects were given the correct original version of a story or printed passage, their memory was still influenced by their initial interpretation of the event. In fact, they remembered their own reproduction more accurately than that of the original even after the latter was repeatedly shown to them. In other words, when we code an event into memory and then construct an account of that event, it is not the details of the actual event that we remember, but the stories we first told ourselves about that event. And what guides our idiosyncratic constructions? Experience. Knowledge. Values. Our mood at that particular moment. Such factors determine what we perceive to be the most essential and resonating details of the event and how we will compress, expand, and reorder those details, sometimes even importing them from beyond the perimeters of the event, and then, how we will package them in a tidy form, dried and frozen but easily reconstituted.

I dismiss neither my great-aunt's nor my grandmother's story because I understand the spirit in which each was told. My grandmother, who had no ethical qualms about getting something for nothing at another's expense, would find no wrong in stealing a little milk, especially if one's family was hungry. Not only would she pronounce the first husband of her favorite aunt, Mary Bunker, not guilty, but she would find such an act downright commendable. My great-aunt Pertsie, with the full dance card and three marriages, would judge a little adultery inspired by one's zest for life far more pardonable than thievery.

The hard remains of memory cannot be transported to the laboratory like the remains of Piltdown man, the reputed missing evolutionary link, and submitted to a series of paleontological tests like those that revealed the fraud (a modern human cranium joined to the jawbone of an orangutan). Often, no evidence remains to corroborate our stories. Montrose is not the boomtown it was in the early years of this century when Ab fiddled or his widow brewed and sold moonshine corn liquor to support her children. And while Montrose is now little more than a few bait shops and a convenience store, the surrounding area is no longer so pristine that willow groves still shade the floodplains. Neither can I return to the setting of my turtle shell memory—the old log house where Pop and Pertsie once lived. It has not remained in the family as homes once did, and even if it had, it would bear little resemblance to the original structure after decades of my great-aunt's amateur remodeling and expansions. Consequently, Pop's room no longer exists as I remember it. Likewise, possessions are so easily and cheaply acquired in this time and place of material plenty that objects once regarded as heirlooms or keepsakes and stored for a lifetime in attics or cellars are now priced to sell at yard sales or deposited in Goodwill boxes. In truth, there is no place to search for the source of some hard remains.

Despite the convincing lack of physical evidence, I still believe there once was a turtle shell that my great-uncle found—riverbank or desert highway, I cannot say—and fashioned into a jewel bowl for his sister. My sole justification for this belief lies with my own felt sense of certainty. Because a felt sense is subjective and intuitive and cannot be verified by the means we have come to trust—it can't, say, be measured, dissected, or converted into a convincing statistic—I feel remiss in offering it as my only means of validation. Yet, in *The Life of the Mind* (1988), neuropsychologist Jason W. Brown assures me that when evaluating the accuracy of memory, the only real basis of assessment lies with the recollector's subjective feelings of completeness and integrity in regard to that memory, since no template exists against which a remembered version of an event can be compared. In fact, Brown contends, something as nebulous and as unprovable as the feeling that "something is missing" is reason enough to suspect the accuracy of a memory. This recognition of incompleteness is similar to the unnerving experience of the simple amnesiac who is aware of her own memory failure. Brown further explains that the configurations we lay down in the course of retrieval produce a state of awareness that allows us to judge the accuracy of our own memories. "Put differently," he concludes, "the judgment is part of the representation, not a critique elaborated through an independent process."

But on the other hand, when a remembered event seems external to and independent of the perceiver, as do hallucinations, then the accuracy of the images is doubtful, says Brown. This means that in the absence of external validation, a reliable memory is best recognized by its subjectivity and by the relation it bears to the life of the recollector. Subjectivity, the very quality that hinders my faith, also bears my only assurance of authenticity.

It doesn't matter how we clothe our bones, whether their threads are locally grown and spun, imported from afar, or woven from the very air, like the emperor's new robes. What matters is memory's lightning-like ability to illuminate the landscape, to bring forth shape and substance from the darkness, if only for a flash. This begetting ability is dependent not on how faithful or fickle our remembrance of the original event is but rather on the clarity with which we see it and the certainty with which we hold it.

My remembered turtle shell reverses time. It reclothes my dead with flesh and sinew and breath. The turtle shell jewel bowl empties itself of its human-made contents, fills again with flesh and scales and breath, turns upright, parts grass. Flesh and bone dissolve and condense into seed, then parents, then seed, again and again. In time, the shell retreats. A slim amphibian slithers into the warm slurry of waters whence it came. Legs become fins; lungs become gills. Bones dissolve until at last the creature is floating, Precambrian, unicellular. A creature who, even then, bears the faint impulse to lay down hard remains.

August 1990

# WILDFLOWERS

When I emerged from the kindergarten classroom into the bright afternoon thirty springs ago, it was not my grandmother I found waiting to walk me home as usual but my grandfather in his new blue Rambler. Instead of heading home by way of the Cozy Corner for milkshakes, he drove north through Keokuk, where we lived at that time, to the Great River Road, a dangerously narrow and neglected highway cut into the bluffs, halfway above the Mississippi, halfway below the sky.

No rod and reel leaned against the back window. No tackle box rattled on the seat. This was simply a joyride, with no end in mind. South of Montrose, Iowa, a village once called Mount of Roses because of the wild sweetbrier pinking its bluffs, was a steeply wooded slope, erupting with wildflowers. "Look!" I pointed. My grandfather eased the car off the shoulderless road and climbed out. "Go get yourself a fistful," he nodded. While he leaned against the side of the car, the lower half of the thicketed bluff, the gray water, the green floodplain of Illinois behind him, I turned to the blooming hill. How could I possess them all?

I snapped stems, reaching for the next one before the fingers of my other hand had yet closed about the last. When my grandfather called me back, I objected: though my hands were full, so many flowers remained. I slid onto the hot plastic-covered seat beside him, gripping the watery stems of the spring beauties; the fragile furry stems of the bluebells; the thicker, firmer stalks of sweet William; of daisy fleabane; of columbine and the arching brown stems of the Dutchman's breeches. Before we even reached the city limits, the stems of my bouquet had begun to lose their starch.

I entered the house bearing my drooping bounty. My grandmother exclaimed her delight as she plunged the stems into a water-filled Kerr jar and then pulled the bouquet loose and full. She centered the arrangement on the dining room table next to a platter of barbecued ribs. We piled clean rib bones and crumpled white napkins, orange with grease and sauce, beside our plates while we watched the flowers wilt by degrees. Bluebells and columbines hung in bruised folds, their blues and scarlets more concentrated than before. The Dutchman's breeches hung like sodden white stockings. "Wild ones just don't keep like ones from the garden," my mother apologized. Not like the ankle-thick bouquets of woody lilacs or the extravagant peonies that scented the house for days. Not like tight rosebuds that opened slowly in tall vases. Not like gold and purple chrysanthemums, the summer's last and hardiest. But in time even those cultivated blossoms browned and shed their petals.

When I entered the dining room the next morning, I felt as if thieves had come in the night and stolen my one object of value. The table was bare, the Kerr jar dry in the drain rack, and the flowers draped over a mound of coffee grounds in the garbage pail. "Just think," my grandmother offered in an attempt to console, "their brothers and sisters will return next spring for you to pick."

But it was not the individual, plucked flower I wanted any longer. What I really wanted to possess was their livingness, that mysterious force that converted sun and soil and rain into shape and scent and hue. What I really wanted was their essence.

Though I could not articulate any of this at the time, I did sense that for the essence to be whole, the flower had to remain unplucked—stem attached to roots, roots attached to earth. Once this link was severed, the flower's essence dispersed.

Years later, I read of the Aztecs, who believed themselves chosen to maintain the life of the sun by feeding it morsels of life essence found only in beating human hearts. Their priests became adept with the obsidian knife. Fifteen thousand hearts per year. As many as eighty thousand in 1487, the year of the temple dedication. But essence dissipates quickly from a disembodied heart. Nearly gone by the time it reaches the altar, with nothing but shadow remaining once essence is parted from that which gives it shape. Once parted, essence becomes amorphous and dispersed. It is subject without form, spirit without flesh, dance without a dancer.

I remember the circumstances of my first bouquet in clearest detail. I remember the surprise of leaving school in my grandfather's new car; the way the hot plastic of the front seat stuck to my bare legs; the spareribs slathered with sauce; the full garbage pail. But, I must confess, I do not remember the flowers so well. In truth, that thirty-year-old bouquet is fleshed out with blossoms I've picked and identified in the meantime. Only the unforgettable Dutchman's breeches, perfectly molded confectioneries, were really there. If I cannot recall the tangible flowers, it is because the tangible flowers were all I possessed: I had failed to perceive their essences.

Ironically, it is a later unpicked field of flowers that I remember in finer detail. The first time I saw a prairie in bloom, I felt its potent but vulnerable presence, a beating heart above, below, and beyond the cut of any knife. The magenta of the purple poppy mallows seized my attention first, followed by clusters of gold prairie groundsel, then colonies of white anemones and wild strawberry blossoms hugging the earth. The lavender blooms of the silver-leafed lead plant demanded a finer focus yet. I was hungry to possess them all; however, the sign at the entrance to Nine-Mile Prairie, just west of Lincoln, forbade me from collecting a single thorny thistle. If I couldn't take the blossoms with me, how was I to preserve the day? Only one way existed, and that was by distilling its essence, by making the eye keen and patient, by making the mind blank and dry, ready to absorb what the eye perceived.

I left the prairie with empty hands, appetite filled to stillness. The spring flowers I beheld that day bloomed long after summer asters and sunflowers rose above them. They bloomed through the prairie winter. They bloom here still, crisp, bright, fragrant, whole.

June 1991

# NATURAL RESISTANCE

*E*ach of my four-year-old daughter's drawings contains a highly arched rainbow, with whatever colors she has—pink, gray, and black, for instance. Last winter, I showed her a photograph of a rainbow and pointed out that the colors are always the same and always in the same order, though certainly her crayoned rainbows did not have to follow such a scheme. She named the colors: red, orange, yellow, green, blue, purple. Violet, I corrected her. The purple in the rainbow is called violet. It is blue-purple, like the petals of the violets that bloom each spring. But she was too young to remember the shape, the color, or the name of the flowers we picked last spring. Wait until May, I told her. We will pick a big bouquet of violets.

This is my last spring in this place and in this family. I am leaving my home of seven years and my husband of five years. My daughter's time will be divided between her two homes, her two parents.

The first step in my leaving came last January when I accepted a teaching position six hundred miles away. My husband's plan, to which I reluctantly consented, was that he and our daughter would remain in Nebraska, my son and I would move to Illinois. Our family would spend holidays, every other weekend, and three months in the summer together. Other academic couples kept their marriages and families intact over even greater distances. We could do it, too. Yet, the very thought of living away from either of my children was agonizing—enough so that several times I came close to giving up the position so I could keep my family together.

My job was not to begin until August, which seemed far away last winter. Then, when thoughts of leaving entered my head, I ignored them. Sufficient unto the day is the trouble thereof. But when spring arrived, the reality of my leaving became hard and near. The impending separation created a rift between my husband and me—or more honestly, it widened a rift that was already there. We talked less and less; our differences lay unresolved. "Only five more months of this," I'd tell myself. "Only four more months." My husband later confessed that he, too, was just "waiting it out." Though we still lived at the same address, we could not have been more apart. By early May, I knew that even if I turned down my ideal job and stayed in Nebraska, my husband and I could never bridge, much less close, the distance that gaped between us. I filed for divorce but prayed for miracles.

I am sad about all that I will be leaving. I am sad about leaving the gardens I've planted, weeded, and harvested; about leaving the cedar tree beneath which my cat died; about leaving the forsythia bush beneath which I buried an eight-week-old fetus (more seahorse than human, it seemed) that I miscarried two springs ago; about leaving the cottonwoods in this neighborhood with which I am on speaking terms; about leaving the tag-ends of wildness I have discovered within and beyond the city limits. Despite the dissension between my husband and me, I once loved him and still do. During our final weeks together as we wait our court date and my moving date, I find myself recalling not the emotional, spiritual, and intellectual divorces we endured, and might not have had to endure if I had been more generous and willful and if my husband had been more generous and yielding, but those times I felt truly wedded to him.

Most of all I grieve that my daughter—who once swam and rolled in my belly like a fish; who drank milk made by my own flesh; whose round, brown body I wash every evening; who looks at me with my own eyes; who loves my son, her half brother, as he loves her—will spend as many days away from me as with me. Fear churns my stomach. I cry too easily. Dreams of separation awaken me at 3 A.M.

My response to the spring was and is divided. I welcomed the return of the mourning doves and their whistling wings, the organic smell of thawed earth, the muddy shoulders of a country road pulsing with the calls of courting frogs, and the arrival of the first green, more of a suggestion, foretaste, or intuition than anything visible to the eye. But, too, I dreaded the season. The intensity of courting animals reminded me how little resemblance there sometimes is between new love and what follows. Meek violets peeking out from beneath heart-shaped leaves reminded me of how I had failed myself. When I found a bald, blue-bellied nestling dead on the sidewalk, I mourned for its mother, who I imagined also to be mourning. The mourning dove's sad, pulsing notes deepened my sense of loss. As the signs of the season I loved crescendoed toward summer's fullness, I could no longer ignore thoughts of my leaving. While I rejoiced that I had found the will to end what my attorney called an "irretrievably broken marriage," I grieved that my marriage was broken beyond repair.

In her disturbing essay "Against Nature," Joyce Carol Oates says that one reason writers resist nature is because "it lacks a symbolic subtext—excepting that provided by man." Of course this is the very reason so many writers *have* written about nature: it is a mute and blank slate upon which we can so easily impose our own symbolic subtext—something not so easily achieved in the human sphere, since humans sometimes object to what is projected onto them. But when Oates speaks of the writer's resistance to nature, she means not that we avoid nature as the subject of our writing but that we resist *seeing* nature as it is ("Who has looked upon her/its face and survived?" Oates asks). When we see not what is there but what we hope or expect to be there, we have resisted nature.

Theoretically, Oates is correct. A writer can choose whether a violet, for instance, represents grief, rebirth, meekness, assertiveness, modesty, or constancy—the last two, the flower's historical associations. Yet I believe that a responsible nature writer works with real limitations: the metaphors or symbols she projects onto the things of nature must respect the scientific facts. To call the violet meek or timid is to ignore the evidence. Shakespeare referred to the "forward" violet, since he believed that the frail blossom had stolen its bright hue and overbearingly sweet scent. Botanist Peter Bernhardt says that violet blossoms last longer than those of other species and the petals move to different positions (sometimes the flower nods, then is horizontal, then erect) to accommodate a wide variety of pollen-eating and nectar-sucking insects. And too, the violet's seed dispersal strategies are ingenious: exploding seed capsules; tiny edible oil glands that make the seed tasty enough for ants to carry home; and "cryptic" flowers filled with seeds that self-pollinate. To call the violet meek or "shrinking" is to ignore the evidence in favor of what one *wants* to find.

Some critics protest any attributions, whether they are biologically accurate (the "ingenious" and "overbearing" violet) or not (the "shrinking" violet). English art critic and social reformer John Ruskin (1819–1900) says that when a writer ascribes human moods and passions to nature, the writer goes beyond providing a symbolic subtext and indulges in "pathetic fallacies." In *Modern Painters*, Ruskin provides an example of such an excess: "They rowed her in across the rolling foam—the cruel, crawling foam." Though this metaphor (foam crawls like a person or animal) does not violate any facts of science (foam can and does move slowly up the beach), it is inaccurate to say that it is cruel. Since cruelty requires consciousness of one's intentions and only humans possess such an awareness, only humans can be cruel. When a coyote brings down a pronghorn, the coyote is not being cruel; she is driven by an instinctive response to hunger rather than by the *desire* to inflict pain or suffering. Likewise, when *Zenaida macroura* issues his call, he is not grieving, as his common name "mourning dove" would have us believe. He is simply calling to his mate or defending his territory. The mournfulness was in the ear and the mind of the observer who named him, though I confess, this season the dove's call notes sound mournful to me, too. Ruskin explains, "The state of mind which attributes to it [the foam] these characters of a living creature is one in which the reason is unhinged by grief. All violent feelings have the same effect. They produce in us a falseness of external things, which I would generally characterize as the pathetic fallacy."

The assumption that the things of nature are but instruments for my own self-expression is easily understood. Intense emotions may seem so much more than the Self can contain that they spill into the surroundings—especially into the unprotesting natural world. A notable example of what Ruskin identified as our tendency to create the "falseness of external things" is Walt Whitman's description of the hermit thrush in his elegy for Abraham Lincoln, "When Lilacs Last in the Dooryard Bloom'd." This "shy and hidden bird" withdraws to the secluded recesses of the swamp, where he sings a

> Song of the bleeding throat,
> Death's outlet song of life, (for well dear brother I know,
> If thou wast not grateful to sing thou would'st surely die).

A thrush is not shy, and birds do not necessarily die if they cannot sing, though the person observing the bird might feel this way. Nor does the bird sing "the carol of death, and a verse for him I love," as Whitman's speaker believes. Such a statement contradicts biology, which tells us that birds vocalize not to express human emotions but to communicate with other birds through alarm notes, location notes, greeting notes, intimidation notes, food calls, gathering calls, and breeding songs.

Whitman's speaker moves from hearing the thrush's song as an expression of deepest grief to hearing it as a "carol of joy." Death is not something to fear but a part of nature that we should welcome and celebrate as certainly as we do birth, growth, and reproduction. Indeed, death is half of the rhythm of life. Whitman's speaker invites "lovely and soothing death, / [to] Undulate round the world, serenely, arriving, arriving, / . . . to all, to each." In the resolution of the poem, the speaker sees the thrush as a symbol of immortality, whose song is "a chant of fullest welcome" for death, the "Dark mother always gliding near with soft feet." This is a liberating and consoling realization for the speaker. Yet, if the speaker is to complete his progress toward acceptance of the natural world, he must move beyond consolation and divest the thrush's song of human emotions. He must hear the thrush's song as an object of beauty in its own right. He must see that the thrush is not singing of death; it is simply singing.

It might seem that one who ascribes human moods and passions to wild things has a desirable attitude toward nature. To hear my grief or joy in the bird's song or to see the violet as a symbol of endurance or assertiveness or any other qualities I wish I did or did not possess is to say that the natural world is inseparable from me—an extension of myself. If this is true, then my attitude toward myself (respect, disdain, ambivalence) will be my attitude toward nature and will determine how I treat the natural world. If I love myself and see the forest as an extension of myself, for instance, then I cannot participate in the nonessential harvesting of trees, and so I cancel my subscription to the daily newspaper, since 90 percent of the paper it is printed on is virgin stock.

Yet seeing nature as part-of-me is a human-centered perspective, which fails to respect the Otherness of the things of nature. D. H. Lawrence attacked William Wordsworth for attempting to melt down a primrose "into a Williamish oneness." Wordsworth didn't leave the primrose "with a soul of its own. It had to have *his* soul. And nature had to be sweet and pure, Williamish. Sweet-Williamish at that! Anthropomorphized! Anthropomorphism, that allows nothing to call its soul its own, save anthropos." (Emphasis mine.) For Wordsworth, nature is not nature but a mirror reflecting Wordsworth's own face.

To deny a thing of nature its separate identity and right to existence is to

judge the other as subordinate to oneself. In the words of Aldo Leopold, such
an attitude reveals a lack of "intellectual humility." It means seeing oneself not
as "plain member and citizen" of the land community (soils, waters, plants, and
animals) but as conqueror of that community. Such an attitude easily permits
other crimes against nature: replacing native with nonnative species, re-routing
rivers, supporting a national petroleum addiction at all costs, poisoning our
own food supplies. It is an approach to nature that is ultimately deadly for all.

If Self and Other form a true marriage in which both parties are equals, the
human not only sees herself in the natural world but also sees the natural world
in herself. When she watches a bee pollinating a flower, she is concentrated.
When she feels a thunderstorm forming, she is unsettled, edgy. When she sees
songbird habitat uprooted for another office building and too many acres of
parking spaces, her words are the outlet for the warbler's grief. Yet I must admit that sometimes, as soon as I see my too familiar face in the leaves or the
ripples, I turn away, disengaging myself from the dialogue, and so the circuit is
not completed. Sometimes, I am like the nineteenth-century orchid hunters,
who ventured into the wilderness not to catch glimpses of the Self but to possess the exotic Other.

To stop resisting nature means seeing it clearly and completely. To dissolve
the boundaries between Self and Other for the purpose of making the Other
into one's own image is to conquer and exploit. To dissolve the boundaries for
the purpose of gaining the perspective of the violet, thrush, or forest reveals respect for the Other. When we respect the Other, we honor and preserve its
selfhood, as we would have our own selfhood honored and preserved. Then, we
have accepted nature.

In May, my daughter and I found hundreds of violets in her preschool play-
ground. She was disappointed by the tiny, pale flowers. She had expected the
long stems and big, crayon-bright petals of tulips, jonquils, and peonies. I was
disappointed too. Instead of rejoicing in their subtle beauty, this spring, I saw
the five-petal faces as sad, heavy-jowled, tear-streaked.

We kneeled to study the blossoms—close enough to see the individual
grains of gold pollen. Not tear-streaked faces, but petals streaked with yellow
and dark-purple nectar guides. Not hung heads, but crooked stems. No matter
how "unhinged" I was by my grief, I resisted my impulse to rework the violet
into a symbol of those qualities I want to find in myself—strength, adaptability,
and regeneration. The violets and I *are* connected, but only in an elemental
sense. As Dylan Thomas once observed: "The force that through the green fuse

drives the flower / Drives my green age." To see this link is to see the natural world. To see more than that is to see what is not there.

My daughter asked if she could pick a bouquet. No, I said. Let's leave the violets in the earth, so they may keep growing and making food for insects. She agreed. Two mourning doves picking gravel in the driveway cooed a low, throbbing *ooah-ooo-oo-oo*. They rose into the air with a whistling of their wings and were gone.

May 1995

# SEEING 'POSSUM

*One usually regards the tail of an animal as a more or less ornamental appendage that is of little use to its owner except as a fly-whisk, but such is not always the case.*
W. S. BERRIDGE, F.Z.S., *Marvels of the Animal World*

S een from my bedroom window, the driveway is a still, silent river. A low, waddling, gray-white animal leaves the far bank, crosses the water, and dissolves into night shadows. The next morning, my fingers trace star-shaped prints pressed in mud.

I've been reading about opossums. Initially, I read simply to verify what I thought I saw and to fill in details I'd missed in that ten-second exposure. But I continue reading because I've become obsessed with the opossum's long and fabulous history of not being seen. By this I do not mean that she is rare and elusive or limited in range. On the contrary, the opossum is prolific (two or three litters per year, five to thirteen per litter), conspicuous (take a midnight stroll through any residential area, along any creek bank, or scan roadkill the morning after), and highly adaptable (she calls any hole-in-the-wall home, she is weatherproof, she is the ultimate omnivore). Rather, when I say that the opossum has a long history of not being seen, I mean that when people looked at her, they often failed to see her as she is.

Take, for instance, the opossum's tail, something that escaped my notice when I had my chance to see. From specimens I have since studied, I can conclude that the opossum's tail is nowhere near as interesting as the beaver's pat solution, the fox's billowing afterthought, the pheasant's sweeping retinue, or the snapping turtle's crusty summation. The opossum's tail is, quite simply, round, thin, and long—nearly half her body length in fact. The third nearest the body is black; from that point to the tip, it is pink or yellow-white. Short, sparse hairs sprout from the scaly surface.

This simple tail has been the subject of nearly five centuries' worth of fanciful stories and drawings that read more like science fiction or fantasy than the natural history they claim to be. The first known illustration of the opossum by a European graces the lower left-hand corner of Martin Waldseemüller's 1516 world map. The animal it depicts, identified as an opossum by description rather than by name, is, to my eyes, a cocker spaniel with a thick neck, shaggy fur, a trunk high off the ground, and a bobbed tail. This must have seemed accurate to other mapmakers too—the same illustration appears on the 1552 Ptolemy map with one slight variation: the Ptolemy opossum faces the east instead of the west.

Even more fantastic is Father André Thevet's "su," one of the beasts of the "New Founde Worlde" that he described in his 1557 *Les Singularitez de la France antarctique*. Not only does Thevet's monster sport a hornless, bearded satyr's head, a greyhound-high belly, the lion's retractile claws, and other very un'possumlike features, but the tail is plumed and arched over its back, sheltering the half dozen or so man-beasts hunched in its shade. The su, identified as the New World opossum, was eventually dismissed as pure invention, but not before it was copied in toto in other "scientific" texts, namely, Konrad Gesner's *Historiae animalium* (1551–58) and the Reverend Edward Topsell's 1658 history of beasts and serpents, in which he described this "cruel, untamable, impatient, violent ravening and bloudy Beast" as "carrying her young ones upon her back, and covering them with her broad tail."

It was not just the shape and length of the tail that the Old World naturalists failed to see, but some overlooked another obvious feature: the tail only curls downward. Opossum expert Carl G. Hartman regards the upward curling of the tail as the harbinger of imminent death, yet the illustrations in some texts,

George Shaw's important *General Zoology, or Systematic Natural History* (1800), for instance, show the tail curling upward. I wonder if the only models permitting close observation were those about to give up the ghost.

In addition to the appearance of the tail, observers often failed to see the ways in which it was used. The tail is prehensile or grasping, what Ernest Thompson Seton calls a "behind hand." In this fifth hand, the opossum rolls leaves, hay, and twigs and transports them to her nesting site. Some mammologists also suspect that the tail functions as a sensor or tactile organ, since the opossum touches the tip to the ground as she ambles along. And, of course, she can hang from her tail. John James Audubon observed an opossum gripping the limb of a persimmon tree with her tail and hind feet and sometimes only with her tail, her body swinging in the air as she gathered the sweet fruit with her front legs.

While this arrangement may be downright efficient, it is also quite unlikely. Hartman explains that the tail is prehensile because the muscles on its underside are strongly developed and well supplied by stout blood vessels. The main purpose of the grasping ability for the opossum and for other tail-grippers— tree porcupines, anteaters, rats, mice, and some monkeys—is to provide additional support. If the opossum loses her footing, the tail grip is the safety belt that prevents her from plummeting to the ground. Yet often naturalists depict the opossum hanging head down from a branch like a glass Christmas bulb, as if this were her preferred and natural position. Some even claim that she sleeps in this unrestful manner. Moreover, in *Pouched Animals*, Frank E. Wood reports that the opossum can hang from a twig or pole by as little as 5 percent of her tail. When you consider the weight of an average opossum (the female that Audubon observed was twelve pounds), the unlikeliness of Wood's claim is evident. Since the ratio of tail strength to total body weight decreases as the opossum grows, the ability to hang headfirst declines with age. Thus, any adult opossum caught hanging from her J for more than a moment or two was probably posed by the wildlife photographer, the artist, or the taxidermist.

But the most curious legend concerning the opossum's tail originated with the Dutch Maria Sibylla de Merian, who painted the tropical plants, insects, and butterflies of Surinam and Dutch Guyana. On the last copper plate in her 1717 *Historie générale des insectes de Surinam et de toute l'Europe* (my caption: "What's Wrong with This Picture? Circle the Mistakes"), Merian represents the life cycle of praying mantises: baby mantises emerge from egg-studded shelf fungus on the underside of a branch to join their progenitors above. In the open space below, Merian positions a mother opossum and her brood. The fact that the opossum is only a nose larger than the mantises and the fact that the opossums' tails are white with widely spaced black rings should alert the viewer to the possibility of other errors: birds with antennae, snakes with legs, fish out of water.

Even more curious than these inaccuracies is the manner in which Merian's mother opossum transports her brood. "When the mother goes out in search of food," the artist writes, "the young follow and when they have eaten or are in a state of fear they jump on the mother's back, twist their tails about hers, and she carries them thus to her nest." In truth, the mother opossum does lug her young on her back from the time they emerge from the pouch at sixty-seven days until they are ready to venture off on their own a few weeks later. Yet to secure themselves, as Hartman tells it, they grasp the thick fur of the mother's head, neck, back, or legs with their claws and wrap their tails around any available body parts—which may or may not be the mother's tail.

Unfortunately, this error-riddled plate in Merian's book remained the European authority on opossums for the next two centuries. Carolus Linnaeus, the ambitious eighteenth-century classifier of all earthly life, lifted Merian's description of the New World beast for his *Systema Naturae* (1735), christening it *Didelphis dorsigera*—"di" meaning double; "*delphis*," womb (a surprising accuracy, since the opossum possesses two uteri unless Linnaeus considered the pouch one of these wombs); and "*dorsigera*" meaning back carrier, in recognition of Merian's discovery. Of this creature, Linnaeus writes: "Inhabits Surinam; burrows in the ground; brings five or six young, which when in danger stick to the back of the mother, twisting their tails around hers."

But as with the childhood party game Telephone, Merian's tail-gripping tail myth proves just how distorted and embellished a message can become through subsequent retellings. By the time it reached the twentieth century, this peculiar South American mode of securing the young that Merian claims to have witnessed had not only extended to the Virginia opossum, the species now found throughout the continental United States, but it had developed a most amazing twist. A silhouette in H. E. Anthony's *Field Book of North American Mammals* (1928) shows two baby opossums hanging by their tails from their mother's arched tail. A third baby clings slothlike to the very tip with his four feet. A fourth rides aloft. While Anthony makes no verbal claims about the prodigious ability of the opossum's fifth hand, Alan Devoe does. In *Speaking of Animals* (1947), he reports: "Now and again, when she arches her tail, squirrel-fashion, over her back, they wrap the tips of their own tails around and hang from it upside-down." A tail the circumference of the opossum's would need steel reinforcements if it were to support the weight of an average litter of eight or nine.

Old World naturalists committed other grave anatomical errors, but they are more forgivable since they concern less-visible body parts. Repeatedly, these observers claimed to have seen the pouch, often depicted as a balloon or a goiter hanging from the chest, separate from the teats, which were positioned lower on the belly. If nature imitated science, then the immature young, born only twelve days and eighteen hours after conception and smaller than peas, would have to migrate from the pouch to the teats over a mighty wide and rugged terrain for their nourishment. In truth, twelve mammae form a circle on the floor of the pouch, with a thirteenth in the middle, and the pouch is but a flap of skin that the young cannot leave until at least nine weeks after conception.

Uncertainty also surrounded how the newly born, what Blumenbach called "veritable abortions," what Dr. Benjamin Smith Barton called "not foetuses but gelatinous bodies," became attached to the teats. Barton theorized that there were two types of opossum gestation: uterine and mammary. The second method must have seemed logical to Geoffry St. Hilaire; in 1819, he speculated that the embryos were born attached to the mother's teats, which were everted from inside the belly. "Though contrary to the Laws of Nature," says Mark Catesby, a Royal Fellow and author of a New World natural history (1741), "nothing is more believed in America than that these Creatures are bred at the Teats by their Dams." Dr. Willem Piso and Georg Marcgrave went so far as to state that the semen was received in the pouch and the young formed therein. Even among those scientists who acknowledged the presence of a uterus or two, there existed the belief that a direct passage linked the uterus and the teats. Moreover, reputable scientists such as Charles César Rochefort, who wrote a seventeenth-century natural history of the West Indies, and Robert Kerr, the eighteenth-century naturalist and member of the Royal College of Surgeons, endowed the male opossum with teats and a pouch also so that he and the female could share duties.

Eventually, someone conceived of dissecting a pregnant opossum to learn how and from where the young made their entrance. Catesby wrote of a Dr. Tyson, who discovered through anatomization that since "their Structure is formed for Generation like that of other Animals, they must necessarily be bred and excluded the usual Way of other Quadrupeds." Audubon also dissected, paying slaves on neighboring plantations to obtain pregnant specimens for his studies. But no one reports having witnessed an opossum giving birth until Audubon's friend, Dr. Middleton Michel, did so in 1847, and he observed only the actual exclusion, not the migration to the pouch. These dissections and close observations revealed that the female delivers about twenty fetuses from her double uterus through a single birth canal while in a sitting position.

She then licks the fetuses to release them from the close-fitting, fluid-filled amnion, in which they would otherwise drown. Once freed, the babies climb the three inches to the pouch (since only the front paws are clawed at this point and since the mother is inclined, the only way to go is up), where thirteen attach themselves to the pin-size nipples and the rest perish.

This licking also led to wild speculation, namely, that the mother lifts the babies from her cloacal opening with her mouth and drops them in the pouch. Audubon, for instance, said he saw a mother shove the newborns into the pouch "and with her nose or tongue move them in the vicinity of the teats." The licking action coupled with the fact that the male's penis is forked led to the wildest theory of all: that the female conceives through her nostrils—two openings—and sneezes her minute offspring into her pouch. James F. Keefe, an information officer for the Missouri Department of Conservation, wrote in 1967 that he still received frequent written inquiries asking him to confirm or deny the theory.

I can explain some of these inaccuracies. Those who wrote of the opossum weren't necessarily those who had seen it, and that is sloppy scholarship. Since the opossum's range was confined to what for Europeans was the New World—the Americas, Australia, Tasmania—few Old World naturalists observed the creature in its natural state. If they saw the opossum at all, it was most likely a New World souvenir grown fat, infertile, and lazy in captivity. A mere shadow of the real thing. The German Konrad Gesner, for instance, regretted that his sketch and description of the opossum was based entirely on the authority of others . . . who may or may not have seen the animal themselves. The Reverend Edward Topsell, the English clergyman and armchair naturalist who wrote "to passe away the Sabaoths in heavenly meditation upon earthly creatures," gleaned his facts from Gesner, Thevet, and others. The Spaniard Vicente Yáñez Pinzón, captain of the *Niña* and leader of his own three expeditions to the Americas, was the first European known to have seen the "incredible mother" with her pocketful of young, yet it was not he but the Venetian Peter Martyr who wrote of this first marsupial encounter in his 1516 *De Orbe Novo*. Peter Martyr—who never left the Old World, much less saw an opossum. In other words, the first written account was already once removed. Not "drawn from nature," as Audubon promises on each of his lithographs.

Being wrong about the appearance of something we've never seen isn't such a wonder. Being wrong about what lies before us is. The Dutch Piso and Marcgrave, credited with being the first scientists to systematically study the flora and fauna of South America, had abundant opportunities to study members of the genus *Didelphis*. Piso even performed a dissection on an opossum in the

1640s—the earliest recorded dissection, to my knowledge—after which he concluded: "The pouch is the uterus of the animal, it has no other, as I have determined by dissection."

Even the observant and often accurate Audubon, himself highly critical of the "vulgar errors" circulating about opossum reproduction, appears not to have seen the specimens prowling his plantation on moonlit nights. In *Quadrupeds of North America*, Audubon—or perhaps his friend John Bachman, who wrote for him in later years—notes: "The gait of the Opossum is slow, rather heavy, and awkward; it is not a trot like that of the fox, but an amble or pace, moving two legs on one side at a time." Other naturalists also professed to have seen the opossum "single-footing," as Elliott Coues termed it in *The Fur-Bearing Animals of North America* (1877). But animal locomotion expert A. Brazier Howell explained in a personal communication to Hartman that the opossum is too broad in the beam, too short-legged to single-foot: "Turtles, iguanas, opossums, badgers, are obliged to be well supported and cannot be shifting the center of gravity from side to side, in the pace or amble, as can a narrow one, or one with long legs. Hence opossums trot, even at the slowest tempo."

Then, there is the matter of whether the pouch is located on the chest, separate from the teats, or the nipples are on the floor of the pouch. Martyr's account of Pinzón's encounter with the opossum assures that "many observations have shown that this animal carries its young in the sack of the belly wherever it goes and never lets them out except to suckle them or otherwise refresh them until they are grown." Many observations? Just what was Martyr—or rather, Pinzón—looking at?

Hans Stade was the rare early observer who saw the pouch and teats as they really are. In his autobiography, *The Captivity of Hans Stade of Hesse, in A.D. 1547–1555, Among the Wild Tribes of Eastern Brazil*, he reports that when the "serwoy" breeds, it bears about six young, and it has a slit in the belly, about half a span in length. Within the slit there is yet another skin; for its belly is not open, and within this slit are teats. Wherever it goes, it carries its young in the slit between the two skins. I have often helped to catch them, and have pulled the young ones from out of the slit." But Stade stops short of observational impeccability because he fails to see the tail during such intimate contact. To Stade, the serwoy has a tail like a cat. And apples look like oranges, too.

Descriptions by early European naturalists suggest an explanation for their not seeing the opossum. In the German translation of Martyr's version of Pinzón's encounter with the "frightful animal," it possessed "a muzzle like a fox, a tail like a monkey, ears like a bat, and human hands similar to those of monkeys." Richard Eden, who embellished upon Martyr's account of Pinzón's observation for *The Decades of the Newe Worlde or West India* (1555), wrote:

"Emonge these trees is fownde that monstrous beaste with a snowte lyke a foxe, a tayle lyke a marmasette, eares lyke a batte, handes lyke a man, and feete lyke an ape, bearing her whelpes abowte with her in an owtwarde bellye much lyke unto a greate bagge or purse." Finally, Captain John Smith's description in *True Relation* (1608) endows the opossum with the head of a swine, the tail of a rat, and the size of a house cat.

A tail somewhat like a monkey's in that it curls under. Yet monkey tails are fleshier and fur-covered. Somewhat like a rat's in that it is long, thin, and nearly hairless, yet the opossum's tail is not as long nor as thin nor as hairless, proportionally speaking, and certainly the coloration is not the same. With a double bend of the imagination, one can see the opossum's tail as somewhat like the marmoset's—except that the marmoset's is bushier, striped, and very, very long. Somewhat like, but not exactly.

When the Old World naturalists beheld that which made the New World new to them, they saw it in terms of the old. J. Robert Oppenheimer once said that it is the conservative nature of scientific inquiry—nay, of the human mind—that demands that we approach the new through the familiar and old-fashioned. Moreover, we cannot be surprised or astonished at something unless we have an idea of how it ought to be, and that means seeing similarities. After all, how can the opossum's pouch and tail astonish if we haven't seen and can't recall plenty of pouchless creatures for whom the tail is little more than an ornamental appendage or a ready fly whisk? Thus, our *only* means of approaching the new, whether in science or in our wider travels, is via the known: "It is the freight with which we operate: it is the only equipment we have," Oppenheimer asserts.

So, when British colonist John Lawson ate his first dish of 'possum, he compared the taste and texture to that of pork and veal, which it is not. When Captain John Smith described the opossum, he compared her pouch to a "bagge"; for Audubon, it was a "pocket"; for Eden, a "purse." But the pouch is none of these things. And, too, the similarities that these early naturalists perceived determined how they spoke of the beast, which in turn determined how they would continue to see it. Konrad Gesner, for instance, fashioned the first European name for the New World wonder—simiavulpina—from Pinzón's description of the "half monkey, half fox." For Pinzón, the opossum's hind feet called forth images of monkeys, since the new creature possessed large, opposable thumbs. Of course, this welded name made Thevet's illustration particularly appropriate for Gesner's text, since the "su" has a plume for a tail and the tiny beasts riding on the mother's back are crouched in a simian manner. But the opossum is neither monkey nor fox, and certainly there are other creatures it more closely resembles. Minks, skunks, muskrats, and ermines, for instance.

Yet Gesner used what equipment he had. So, too, did the others who bestowed comparative names on the New World animal mirabile: *rat de bois* to the eighteenth-century French explorers; *comedreja*, or weasel, to the Argentineans of the Rio de la Plata; *micuré*, or little pig, to the Paraguayans; *zorro*, or fox, to the Central American Spaniards. Fortunately, the common name by which we now know the *Didelphis* is the purely descriptive one that Smith learned from an Algonquian-speaking relative of Pocahontas. "Opassum," as Smith spelled it in his 1612 *Map of Virginia*, means simply "white beast."

If recognizing similarities and differences between the new and the familiar is our only means of grasping what is otherwise too slippery and new to handle, then it is eye-opening. For explorers from Europe and the eastern United States, the region between the Missouri and the Rockies was a desert: it was uninhabited, uncultivated, barren, treeless, and, in some places, sandy. To see that the region lacked those things that the Old Worlders associated with good and desirable land was the starting point for vision. But for those whose inner eye shut and sealed after this first recognition ("We rode for some five or six miles, and saw no living thing but wolves, snakes, and prairie-dogs," Francis Parkman notes somewhere in Nebraska), then comparing the new with the known was deadening, since it kept the viewers from seeing that there was water enough for the prairie's many thriving inhabitants. That is, if bison, people, pronghorns, cottonwoods, dung beetles, larks, and bluestem count for anything.

I, too, know the blinding influence of first comparisons and the sticky lasting labels that adhere to the face of things. Though I have studied the three books listed under "opossum" in the university library card catalog (I will confess that I got no further than the title of the third: *The Systematics of the Genus Didelphis*); though I have tracked down the other books and articles dealing with opossums that were not cataloged under that identifier; though I have taken advantage of my night wakefulness to survey the driveway for infrequent return engagements; and though I have inspected road-killed opossum for the finest details, the creature is still a rat. Say "'possum," and I see rats transmuting into 'possums, transmuting into rats, transmuting into 'possums like a hologram portrait I transform with the tilt of my head: Christ knocking, Christ opening the door; Elvis musing pensively, Elvis caught midswivel.

I have nothing to lose in seeing the opossum as she is. Still, I can't unstick the label that keeps announcing my first impression. How much harder would it be to see 'possum if I did have something at stake?

Perception of the new muddles the small, tidy order we have made of our observations. So much so that we'll seek the slimmest, most tenuous strands of evidence if they reinforce the order we've imposed, if they corroborate our cosmologies. For the credulous Columbus, confirmation came in the form of a few shared syllables. When he heard his sailors refer to the West Indians as "Caniba," he was certain they were speaking of the Khan he sought because of the shared consonant and vowel sounds. Furthermore, when he asked the Anawak Taino Indians of Cuba where "Cipango" or Japan lay, they pointed east to Haiti, answering "Cibao," thinking that it was the so-named mountain range that he wanted. One more shared syllable and Columbus had the verification he needed: his literal worldview was correct. Forget that the Great Khan had been dead for nearly two centuries. Forget that what appeared before Columbus's physical eyes differed markedly from the elephants, camels, palm trees, Italianate castles, and round-eyed, fair-haired Chinese he might have seen in the fourteenth century *Book of Marvels* illumination of the Far East that Marco Polo supposedly encountered. Columbus read the evidence not for what it was but for what he wanted it to be. In accommodating the facts to his faith, how much of the New World did he fail to see? And if he had unsealed his inner eye and surveyed what stretched before him, what major revisions in his literal worldview would that have exacted?

In a letter to fellow scientist Charles Thomson, Thomas Jefferson acknowledged the universal tendency to select and ignore evidence: "The moment a person forms a theory, his imagination sees, in every object, only the traits which favor that theory." So, if one believes the New World inferior to the Old, every species he meets will confirm that belief. If one believes that the New World and its inhabitants are just waiting to be owned and used, then the eye will close toward evidence to the contrary. If one believes there really is nothing new under the sun, then the inner eye will reshape the evidence until only the familiar appears. What we believe, we see.

This reshaping tendency also occurs in the thousands of more mundane theories we postulate each day. The way this works in our moment-to-moment acts of perception, according to Stephen Grossberg of Boston University, is that what we see activates a feedback process "whereby a learned template, or expectancy, deforms the sensory data until a consensus is reached between what the 'data' are and what we 'expect' them to be. Only then do we 'perceive' anything." Rarely is our vision completely faithful; rarely is it completely creative. Rather, we occupy a perceptual middle ground where the data act upon us and we upon them.

But distinctions exist between the inhabitants of this middle ground and how willingly they reach consensus. Piagetians say that when discrepancy exists between what we must integrate from our experiences and what our present cognitive structures are capable of integrating, conflict exists. Our attempts to regulate these disparities fall into one of three categories. When we display the "alpha" response, we either so modify the disturbing perception that it no longer interferes with our expectations or we ignore that perception altogether. Thus, Dr. Piso's observation over a dissected opossum: "The pouch is the uterus of the animal, it has no other."

When we display the "beta" response, however, we are willing to make some alterations in our current cognitive structures. A little modification here, a little reorganization there. Even so, we do not possess enough new schemes, enough subcategories to accommodate all new experiences. Like those Old World observers—Pinzón, Stade, Thevet, Merian, Audubon—we seek the new but aren't prepared for anything as novel as the opossum. Like those Old World observers, we give an inch when we ought to give a mile.

Finally, when we display the "gamma" response, we receive the world almost as it is because we have constructed a system that allows us through inference to anticipate endless variations. More things in heaven and earth than dreamed of in any philosophy. Show the gamma respondent an opossum for the first time and she won't play dead or transform it into a cat, a rat, or a phantasm. She will see 'possum, pouch and tail and all.

What must we do to become gamma respondents? We could trust evolution, yet many naturally developing people walk tree-lined streets still perceiving every deciduous tree as a lollipop on a stick and every needle-bearing tree as an isosceles triangle because those were their first metaphors and they've not in the intervening decades felt any call to revise or remake their "learned templates." Thus, when they are confronted with an exception to their rule—say, the vase shape of the elm, the symmetrical blade of the poplar, the shook-loose crown of the cottonwood, the parasol top of the palm—they quickly prune and pull the edges until they fit the mold. The Comte de Buffon theorized that New World species, whether native or introduced, were smaller and degenerated compared with their Old World counterparts. When Thomas Jefferson discovered that the great French encyclopedist had neither weighed nor measured nor even seen some of his New World evidence, relying instead upon the reports of Old World excursionists to those far lands, Jefferson demanded: "But who are these travelers? . . . Were they acquainted with the animals of their own country, with which they undertake to compare them? Have they not been so ignorant often to mistake the species?" We cannot say a New World roe or hedgehog or water rat is smaller and less vital than the Old version if our knowledge of one or both is partial, derived from fanciful animal histories, unreliable observers, or our own unseeing eyes. To compare the new to what we do not know, to compare a tree to a triangle when we've only a vague notion about how the latter is shaped, is to know no more than when we began.

Yet to remain too long focused upon the familiar is nearly as deadening as not looking at all. If, for instance, we encounter an opossum for the first time and see that it shares the rat's shoe-button eyes, delicate clamshell ears, short legs, and long, thin tail, clearly our mind's eye is more precisely honed on the stored image than it is on the new. Then what shall we remember when the unseen opossum is itself a stored image? How many other ratlike features will it have acquired in the meantime? When we look for similarities, we must look as carefully at the new as we do at our memory of the familiar. Otherwise, we can turn anything into a rat.

If perception is a negotiation between what is and what we expect it to be, as Grossberg maintains, then the image we form of the Other will always be partial. Yet we can strive toward greater completeness, greater objectivity, and so receive more for our perceptual money's worth in the end. While I know nothing about constructing new cognitive structures, I do believe perception can be made pure and honest and transparent by the heat of discipline. What creates a fire hot enough to burn off the dross is renunciation of our desire to remake the Other in our own images, followed by the accurate translation of that undefiled image into words. Faithful translation insists that we suspend our tendency to reach for metaphor until we are acquainted with both the tenor and the vehicle, with both the new subject and the old to which we are comparing it. To say the opossum's tail is like a monkey's is a venial sin in the world of visual accuracy if we know only the monkey. But to say the opossum's tail is like the monkey's when we know neither animal is to sin mortally.

Faithful translation demands that we travel light. If our Old World tools of discovery—field guides and compasses, slide rules and rules of thumb, hand lenses, specimen crates, and four o'clock tea sets—render us too ungainly to trail the adept night creatures that prowl our riverbanks, too clamorous to slither undetected into the burrows beneath the roots where the day-sluggish sleep, or too weighty to scale our highest trees and tiptoe slim limbs, then we must cast them off, one by one or all at once. As New World travelers in new lands, the only equipment we need when we meet the new is eyes that are always open and a willingness to perceive endless variations. Then, we shall see 'possum, pouch and tail and all.

So. When you behold the opossum, what do you see?

It is Sunday morning and I am the first one about. On the grass between the sidewalk and the street lies a curl of dirty white. I believe it is a wadded rag or a damp crumple of newsprint, but as I near, features form: clamshell ears; a pink snout; V-pointed teeth; a loose tongue, the tip lolling between slightly parted teeth. It is a mouth frozen midsneer, midsnarl, midscream. The tail is an O, but I cannot see where the ends meet or if they do at all, since beginning and ending are lost in grizzled fur. This tail is dusty black at the thick end, dusty pink the rest of its length, or at least as far as I can see. Though the surface is scaled, it is not liquid and moving like some other scaled things: fish, music, snakes, sequined gowns. This tail reminds me of nothing I've seen before, yet it is as familiar as my own skin. This tail. More than an afterthought, a coda, a postscript, a last leg to stand on, it is essential statement, the heart of the matter, a fitting end, the final word.

Fall 1991

# OPEN WATER

*Just as one cannot set out consciously to "construct" symbols,
so one cannot confront a genuine symbol on merely
conscious, rational levels. One must . . . engage it and
struggle with it on all levels of affect and willing.*
ROLLO MAY, "Symbolism," in *Religion and Literature*

We stand in the fresh snow on the river side of Tama Beach Levee, Crossing #6. It is zero degrees, December 27, high noon. Before us lies the Mississippi, white and frozen near the bank, choppy and gray-white in the middle. The north end of O'Connell Island is directly east of where we stand; two smaller islands lie side by side to the north. In the distance on the Illinois side, between O'Connell and the twin islands, are three grain elevators and a mill. O'Connell Slough looks more like a bay than part of the big river.

My son is eagle-eyed. He scans the bare cottonwoods, elms, and ashes between the river and the levee. "There's one," he announces. My eyes follow his finger to a small knot on the far side of the bend. A squirrel nest or a big crow, I suppose.

My mother and I lift our binoculars. A white cap offers immediate confirmation. But even without the white head, the shape of the dark form—broad-shouldered and square—offers all the proof I need that the knot in the tree is not crow or hawk or nest but bald eagle.

We work our way down the beach past a fallen tree and three cabins on twenty-foot stilts, hoping for a closer look at the eagle. Suddenly, he lifts, strokes deeply, and then soars on flattened wings out of sight. The show is over.

But not entirely. When we return to the levee crossing my mother points to a red frill on an elm. "Pileated woodpecker!" she announces. I hear the drumming and see the red crest moving. Though I have never seen this uncommon species, I am more irritated than excited. My eyes and heart are set on eagles, but it is too cold to wait and watch any longer.

I knew little about the bald eagle until I spent a long winter afternoon at the library. The bird experts I found in those few stacks were bent on deciding whether the bald eagle was a wise choice for our national emblem. One of the bird's most outspoken critics was Benjamin Franklin, who lamented the choice of this bird as our representative. In a 1784 letter to his daughter, Sarah Franklin Bache, he wrote that the eagle is "of bad moral character; he does not get his living honestly; you may have seen him perched on some dead tree, where too lazy to fish for himself; he watches the labor of the fishing-hawk, and when that diligent bird has at length taken a fish, and is bearing it to his nest for support of his mate and young ones, the bald pursues him and takes it from him." Stealing food from the mouths of babes, so to speak.

But, too, the bully is a "rank coward," since "the little King-bird, not bigger than a Sparrow, attacks him boldly, and drives him out of the district." Consequently, the fish vulture is not a proper symbol for those who have driven all the kingbirds from their land. Franklin confessed his pleasure that the bald eagle depicted on medals, badges, and seals might easily be mistaken for a turkey, a vain, silly, but courageous bird who "would not hesitate to attack a grenadier of the British guard, who should presume to invade his farmyard with a *red* coat on."

While I do not know how much field experience Franklin had with either eagles or turkeys, I can speak with more certainty of John James Audubon's. He climbed trees to peer into nests; felled trees to capture eaglets; observed hunting strategies through a "good glass" on Florida's St. Johns River, on the Mississippi, on Lake Pontchartrain, on Pennsylvania's Perkiomen Creek; and shot more specimens to study, eat, or paint than I care to think about. But Audubon, too, lamented our choice of a lazy, thieving tyrant as national sym-

bol: "The great strength, daring, and cool courage of this Eagle, plus his un-
equaled power of flight, render him highly conspicuous among his brethren.
Had he a generous disposition towards others he might be looked up to as a
model of nobility."

Still, the bald eagle has champions. Francis Hobart Herrick, whose field experience and meticulous observation of the balds near Vermilion, Ohio, sur-
passes that of any ornithologist I know about, Audubon included ("In tabulat-
ing our records of sixty visits to the eyrie, June 15–30, 1923," Herrick writes, "I
found that the nest-perch was taken forty-three times"), has nothing but praise
for this "undisputed ruler of the sky . . . the emblem of freedom, the incentive
to valor, and pledge of victory." Herrick convincingly defends his monarch
against Franklin's and Audubon's claims that he is but a petty thief. More than
once, Dr. Herrick observed one or two plucky little kingbirds pursuing an old
eagle to its eyrie, "alight at the highest point, and, as the spirit moved, dart with
vim at the great tyrant sitting in unconcern but a few feet away." With each
lunge of the little masked bird, the eagle only opened its mandibles slightly
and, on the whole, seemed rather bored. Such indifference is the eagle's usual
policy. But when a small hawk once tried the same ploy, "it met with a quick
surprise, for after dodging a number of times the eagle opened its talons and
with one thrust instantly stopped the game and barely missed the hawk." Apparently, the eagle can assess which threats are real, which are not, and respond accordingly. Her attitude toward the doughty little kingbird reveals not
cowardice, as Franklin concluded, but discrimination. Likewise, the eagle robs
the osprey only when the latter is "heedless in giving him the chance, or, as it
were, offers him the challenge."

Equal to her discriminating faculties is the bird's remarkable adaptability. The eagle that lives near human settlements only seems complacent and
timid; in truth, she has learned through long and bitter experience that when
humans are involved, circumspection is the price she must pay for her life
and liberty. After all, the eagle is no dodo that would unflinchingly face the
guns and arrows of her human neighbors, becoming extinct as her visage is
reproduced on seals, coins, quilts, totem poles, mastheads, buffalo hides, and
weathervanes. The eagle, Herrick concludes, is a fit symbol for a "strong and
resourceful race."

Brave and cowardly. Tolerant and tyrannical. Discriminating and adaptable.
Were our nation-makers aware that the symbol they had chosen embodied
such contradictions? Perhaps, like Mark Catesby, they didn't look long or hard
enough when they beheld the American eagle. In his *Natural History of Caro-
lina, Florida, and the Bahama Islands* (1754), the English naturalist wrote glow-

ingly though briefly—a mere two hundred words—of this creature of "great strength and spirit," which despite its usual subjugation of other birds, "suffers them to breed near his royal nest without molestation." Perhaps like Arthur Cleveland Bent, Catesby was too dazzled by the eagle's ability "to add grandeur to the scene." And how could one not be impressed by the wicked, hooked beak, the snow-white head, the wild yellow irises ringing the adult's piercing pupils, the inch-long black talons, the breadth of the wings?

I have only witnessed the bald eagle's stillness and grandeur. If I accept Herrick's purple praises or Franklin's and Audubon's condemnations, I must accept them on faith. Perhaps each man's assessment of the eagle is correct: she is both noble and base. She is the bird of contradictions.

December 28. It is twelve degrees above zero at ten o'clock in the morning. The sun shining on the snowy river is blinding. Today my father watches eagles with me. He says we need to find the wing dam, a stone WPA project south of Levee Crossing #6. The dam keeps ice from forming, and open water keeps the eagles alive. If they can't find open water here, they'll seek the warmer waters that separate Missouri and southern Illinois.

Not so long ago, my brother lived in a cabin near the wing dam. Since the east walls in both rooms were lined with windows, spotting eagles was easy. "Do you remember the time an eagle swooped so close you looked him right in the eye?" my mother asks. "No," I answer. Until recently, I had little interest in any type of bird. Besides, eagles are too popular, too recognizable. My interest usually lies with the unsung or understated, which is why I feed blue jays and sparrows all winter.

I drive up and down the beach looking for the wing dam sign. The flood of '93 probably washed it away. My father tries to distinguish which part of the levee used to be the entrance to the cabin by looking for the strip of snow fence my brother laid flat to provide traction on the hill. But snow fences and railroad ties provide a popular foothold along the levee. We find many entrances to my brother's former cabin. Then my son shouts, "Two in one tree!" and we know we have found the wing dam. I park the car and hop out. Even before I lift my binoculars, I can see the closest bird turning her head to look at me.

My son runs to the top of the levee for a closer look. He has spooked the nearest eagle. She courses over the water, wing tips pointed back, endmost feathers spread like fingers, creating a wingspan that eclipses the sun. This image of her outstretched wings, her white head and tail feathers bright against the blue sky, the scimitar-like yellow bill, prompts a parade of associations I do not want: eagles, fierce and vigilant, carved in stone over courthouse and post office doors; spread-winged and perching on the back of the Washington quarter; roosting atop flagpoles; dangling from Boy Scout ribbons; pinned to the shoulder loops of Army generals and Navy captains; mighty and awful amid a squadron of bombers in a World War II Air Corps recruitment poster. The bald eagle: the American bird of freedom.

I'm not even cold or tired, but I call it a day.

Another winter afternoon in the library and I learn that the eagle appealed to the makers of the new United States not because of her natural history but because of her associations with ancient Rome. Despite their claims of separation, these newly emancipated former English subjects were still culturally bound to their ancestral homeland, which was just emerging from a neoclassical revival. The nation-makers modeled their institutions on those of the Roman Republic, choosing for their country's symbol the laurel-wreathed, lightning-bolt-clutching raptor of the Caesars, with all its associations of power, majesty, expansion, and subjugation.

But this symbol did not originate with the Romans. When they adopted it in 104 B.C. (this date is Pliny's), they were merely reworking an already ancient theme. As early as 3000 B.C., according to Herrick's account of the bird's civil history, the eagle was the guardian deity of the Mesopotamian city of Lagash. A Babylonian cylinder unearthed from this period portrays two eagles with wings and talons extended, heads turned to the observer's left, a pose later assumed by the bird on the Roman military standard, "displayed" on European coats of arms and on the Great Seal of the United States.

At this same early date, the double-headed eagle, symbol of sovereignty over east and west, also roosted in Babylonia and in the Hittite city of Pteria. More than an effort at artistic symmetry, says Herrick, the symbol offered, through its omniscience, a "double dose of protection" to those who used it: Belshazzar of Babylon, the Caesars, Charlemagne, many Holy Roman and Byzantine emperors, Napoleon, Russian czars, and some Austrian emperors. Though scholars believe that this ancient symbol may first have arisen among the Babylonians, Herrick suggests that it may have more ancient, less traceable roots in the Neolithic period, making it at least 10,000 years old. Moreover, this bicephalous bird's appeal was not limited to the "cradle of civilization": it adorns the copper work of the Hopewell people, who flourished from 300 B.C. to A.D. 600 in what is now called Ohio, half a world away. Herrick, who places his faith in cultural diffusion, assumes that the double-headed eagle was not the independent creation of the first Americans but rather an Old World symbol conveyed to the New via the Bering Strait migrations.

Also in Babylonia but at a later date, people conceived of the eagle as the bearer of souls, an idea that may have even older African roots. The mythical peasant, Etana, heroically rescued an eagle from the serpent whose young the bird had devoured. In gratitude, the eagle transported his savior to the heavenly abode of the gods. Even though Etana was not well received and was abruptly returned to earth for such presumption, the idea that virtuous souls might reach heaven through the strength and beneficence of this wide-winged bird received a following within and beyond the borders of Babylonia—in Greece, where at Zeus's command, the eagle snatched and bore the golden shepherd boy, Ganymede, to Olympus to become the cupbearer of the gods; in Canaan, where Moses, speaking for Yahweh, declares, "Ye have seen what I did unto the Egyptians, and how I bore you on eagle's wings and brought you unto myself." Interestingly, these different retellings keep alive the entirely inaccurate notion that eagles transport not in their talons but on their backs or wings, which leaves me wondering if the storytellers ever observed an eagle in the wild.

It requires no great leap of logic to see why the eagle came to play such a crucial role in the apotheosis of the Caesars. The Romans believed that a good emperor would return to the daystar, from which he had descended. So, if the people judged their leader worthy of deification, they released an eagle over his burning pyre to symbolize that his emerging soul would not return to the earth, where his body was, but would continue ascending to the heavens. In time, Herrick says, the released raptor no longer symbolized the heavenward flight of the soul, but literally bore it home.

Centuries later, in 1782, William Barton, a skilled draughtsman, herald, and brother of naturalist Benjamin Barton of Philadelphia, submitted to Congress a description of his design for the Great Seal of the United States. It featured a crested heraldic eagle perched on a Doric column (an old symbol of victory over darkness), a flag in one talon and a laurel wreath in the other. Charles Thomson, secretary of the Continental Congress, put his own spin on the design: he exchanged the Old World eagle for the American bald, made the bird more prominent, which meant removing the Doric column, and floated the shield over the bird's entire body (easily achieved, since this specimen is scrawny compared to the one that hovers on our present dollar bills). Thomson's other revisions included replacing the sword, wreath, and flag with an olive branch in the dexter talon and a baker's dozen of arrows in the sinister, the latter a quite Roman revision, since the eagle once bore Jupiter's lightning bolts. Thomson's design for the Great Seal was a "New" World reworking of "Old" World themes. It was approved on September 15, 1789.

It is seventeen degrees at four in the afternoon on December 29. I do not go to Tama Beach today. My father has had another seizure, so I spend most of my day at the hospital.

My father recovers quickly and is unwilling to lie in bed as the doctor ordered. We walk to the east side of the hospital, which provides a bird's-eye view of the river and the floodplains of Illinois since it is built on a high bluff. The old green McArthur Bridge and the suspension bridge that has replaced it keep the water open. About half a mile north and south, the river is solid ice. The frozen river edges form a snowy bank for a narrow rivulet of open water, which looks more like a lake than part of a flowing body of water, half a continent long. It is hard to believe that this stream rose twenty-five feet above normal last summer. Lodged against the ice is a section of the old green bridge that is being floated downriver, where it will be sold as scrap metal.

We pass the office of the director of employee health. She has a splendid view of the river. When I ask if she ever sees eagles, she invites us in for a better look. Just yesterday, she says, she saw the big birds swooping down after gizzard shad. The birds seemed to return empty-taloned, but that is because the shad are only two or three inches long—too small to be seen from this distance. If you come back early in the morning and watch carefully, you can see the birds bring their talons to their beaks as they swing up from the river, the director says. Once sated, the eagles spend the rest of the day loafing on the Illinois side, where there are more trees and fewer people.

Without my son, I can't make out a single white head.

I scavenge the library stacks for anything I can find about how a symbol is made. I learn that the Greek verb *symballein* means "to throw together" and what the representation brings to the point of complete fusion is the specific and the general, the concrete and the abstract, matter and spirit. The fleshly, feathered, and screeching reality of the eagle is one and the same with its mute, airy referent: freedom. Through the symbol, substance and meaning are one.

Theoretically, the symbol-maker has an immense world full of concrete possibilities from which to choose, since anything—blade of grass, darning needle, festering wound, spinning top, cracked egg—can become a symbol under the right circumstances. Moreover, since the range of possible representations from which one may choose is so great, it would appear that a cultural outsider would have only a slight chance of selecting or recognizing an object that is for a particular group both pragmatic and religious—in other words, that weds matter and spirit while imparting concrete traditions as does, say, a Christmas tree topped with a star or the sacred pole of the Sun Dance topped with an eagle's nest.

Christian theologian Paul Tillich says that one of the characteristics of both the secular and the nonsecular symbols is their acceptability as such: they are "socially rooted and socially supported." Even though a symbol may appear to be the conscious creation of an individual, observes Tillich (or a pair of individuals, like Barton and Thomson), it is still a social act. "The individual can devise signs for his own private needs; he cannot make a symbol. If anything becomes a symbol for him, it is always so in relation to the community which in turn can recognize itself in it."

But how does the human community influence what appears to be the individual creation of a symbol? Carl Jung explains that while some of our dream and fantasy images are derived from the day's events, other images are ancient and universal, transcending time, place, and culture. The former images become "signs," analogous or abbreviated expressions of what we already know, but the latter images become living symbols, charged with psychic energy, pregnant with meaning beyond reason's grasp. To illustrate the difference, Jung explains that the sign of a cross after a name on a list simply means that the person has died. But the symbol of the Christian cross expresses "a multitude of aspects, ideas, and emotions," including death and rebirth, psychological maturity, and martyrdom, both for those that bowed before it and for those who would not.

Some symbols are the outward manifestation of what Jung called an archetype, a primordial image that arises in dreams and fantasies, spontaneously, beyond our conscious awareness, just as drives and compulsions arise in the body. The archetype is the psychic correlate of an instinct—a libido analog, if you will.

While the forms of our archetypes are identical, their content is not. "A primordial image," Jung writes, "is determined as to its content only when it becomes conscious and is therefore filled out with the material of conscious experience." Accordingly, the various archetypal symbols that Jung identified—God, trickster, earth mother, hag, eagle, journey, flying saucer, lock and key, and so forth—all initially appeared as "forms without content" but were given substance and definition with details from the dreamer's life, bound as those details are to time, place, culture, and station. For instance, every baby inherits the mother archetype, but individualizes it according to what he knows of his own mother—the shape of her face, her manner of speaking, the nature of the bond between the two, and eventually, the extent to which she fails or meets the maternal expectations of her culture. Universal form, individual content.

Not only is the form of the archetype already determined, but so is its meaning. This is not, Jung emphasizes, because the archetype is an inherited idea, but rather because it is an inherited mode of functioning, every bit as innate as the way an eagle emerges from the egg, constructs her eyrie, hooks a fish, ascends on a thermal. Thus, our collective unconscious does not "consist merely of contents capable of becoming conscious," Jung concludes, "but of latent dispositions towards identical reactions." An archetype is both the organizing principle and the specific image; it is at once stimulus and response.

Consequently, nearly identical responses to the great raptor are found in peoples too geographically diverse for cultural diffusion to explain away the similarities and are far too frequently manifested to be mere coincidence. If drought threatened barrenness and hunger, whether one was Bantu Zulu, Siberian Buriat, Assyro-Babylonian, or Winnebago, it was the whirring of the celestial wings of an eagle or an eaglelike bird that brought thunder, wind, and rain. In a variation on this theme, Oshadagea, the Big Dew Eagle of the Iroquois, carried a lake of dew on his back to restore life on earth after the forces of fire had scorched all vegetation.

If one could not approach the deity on his or her own behalf, the intercessor appeared in avian guise. For the Japanese Ainu, who caged and sacrificed what I guess to be the Steller's Sea Eagle, the great bird spoke to the creator of his captors' needs, of the good treatment he received at their hands, and the people, in turn, were rewarded with cures, fertility, abundance. Some South American Indians represented their shamans or "go-betweens" as harpy eagles—high-flying, carrion-eating mediators who moved freely between the celestial and chthonic spheres. Similarly, the eagle-mediator served as a celestial chariot of both Vishnu and Buddha. Though the association is now nearly buried, Christ, too, was an eagle that plunged to hook souls drowning in a sea of sin, threw the damned out of his nest, bore souls to the chief deity, gazed upon the sun, God's glory, without blinking.

Finally, if darkness and evil threatened humankind, indeed, all creation, in the form of the serpent, the powers of light and goodness, shaped as an eagle and answering to such names as Huitzilopochtli, Marduk, Mithra, Christ, Garuda, Hino, or Odin, grasped the creature in its talons and wrenched the life from it. This ancient drama, in fact, is reenacted each moment on the official emblem of Mexico, where a golden eagle, perched on a cactus, is forever seizing the brilliant green serpent. But in the next chapter of this worldwide tale, the serpent returns and combines with the eagle to form a most amazing hybrid, at home on land, in air, and in sea: the dragon, the plumed serpent, the keeper of the treasure.

Wherever the eagle's shadow skims the land, it speaks to the people of release from that which most oppresses, of exchanging a confining, thwarting way of being for a higher, freer one. Consequently, Barton's choice of the eagle as a symbol wasn't merely the result of his having pored over volumes of heraldic designs, though certainly that influenced his selection of species, pose, and props, but rather, it was the result of his having given shape to some deeply felt, shared impulse. And Barton's instinct did not lead him astray.

December 30 it is twelve degrees and overcast. Before I visit my father at the hospital, I drive past the levee. From the road I see dark buds in the trees across from the wing dam. Two eagles roost in a tree near me, six in a tree an eighth of a mile away. The 1989 Audubon Christmas Bird Count listed only eighty-two eagles in the Burlington area, all of which were concentrated around Lock and Dam 18, north of O'Connell Island. But in the four warm winters since, the numbers of overwintering eagles have climbed. Still, the eight that I observe represent a fair percentage of the total local population.

When I draw near, the closest two lift with a mighty push and settle down-river. Though I have never seen an eagle carry anything in her talons, much less on her back, I can imagine her transporting me heavenward. Through the binoculars I watch one bird land, wings pulled close over her back, feet extended, like a parachuter preparing to meet the earth.

After an evening at the library reading American history, I conclude that several practical reasons confirmed our nation-makers' choice of the eagle as national symbol as much as did the eagle's long history of symbolic significance.

First, the bald eagle was "a true original native," as Franklin stipulated, though it is curious that this fact mattered—indigeneity wasn't valued in other respects. Our "natural aristocrats," for instance, were all European extracts, and it would be a long century and a half before citizenship would be extended to indigenous peoples. Leadership was even further away. Nonetheless, the imperial eagle of European heraldry was disqualified after his brief appearance in Barton's first draft. The golden eagle, equally at home in Europe, Asia, and North Africa, was also disqualified, though in Arthur Cleveland Bent's judgment, he is a "far nobler bird in every way."

Second, the bald eagle was a common, recognizable feature of the American landscape. When Old Worlders first arrived on this continent, eagles bred throughout the Lower Forty-Eight, in most of Canada, Alaska, and northern Mexico. Jon M. Gerrard and Gary R. Bortolotti estimated that at the time of contact, the bald eagle population was a quarter million to a half million strong. This meant that most eighteenth-century Euro-Americans had seen an eagle. Moreover, she wasn't the type of bird they would confuse with others, including her kin—hawks, vultures, ospreys, falcons—except in her immature form when she lacked the distinctive white head and tail.

Of course, New England's woods, clearings, and shores were busy with other common, recognizable birds: gulls, partridges, orioles, whippoorwills, coots, hummingbirds, jays, and pileated woodpeckers, to name but a few. However, a blue jay as a national symbol is laughable not because she is lacking beauty (the crest and bright-blue and white bars are positively regal) or desirable traits (she is smart, brave, aggressive, tenacious, fertile, and a gifted mimic) but because she is too small, too abundant, and her habits are too well known. Since the eagle did not nest in the backyard oak, most people only knew her most salient features—might, beauty, and the height at which she flew. From such a distance, most people hadn't the opportunity to observe either her most admirable or her most offensive traits.

Third, for the eagle to function as a symbol, she had to evoke those qualities that most people associated with the referent. To be free is to know no restrictions on one's actions or movements. Yet when Henry David Thoreau was jailed for refusing to pay taxes to a government that permitted slavery, he proclaimed: "If there was a wall of stone between me and my townsmen, there was a still more difficult one to climb or break through, before they could get to be as free as I was. I did not for a moment feel confined." Say what you want about Thoreau's one-night imprisonment and speedy, anonymous bailout, but because he hadn't the liberty to select the time, place, and substance of his evening fare or to take a constitutional if he chose, the physical person was not free. Because Thoreau had not submitted either unwillingly or unthinkingly to any authority beyond himself, his inner person remained unbound. Freedom from external or physical controls may be a necessary condition of the free person, yet it tells only part of the story, for true freedom also demands release from those "mind-forg'd manacles" of which William Blake wrote. Anything less is just another form of bondage.

To be a perfect symbol of freedom, then, the eagle not only must be common and recognizable but also must summon images of liberation of body and mind. To imagine how completely the eagle once did this, we must forget for a moment the extent to which people and powers control the nineteenth- and twentieth-century bird. We must forget that as early as the 1820s, Audubon noted that eagle populations had diminished because the game on which they preyed had sought refuge deeper in the wilderness to escape human persecution. We must forget that by 1952, the year legal protection extended to Alaskan balds, 128,000 pairs of eagle legs had been turned in for bounties, since the birds preyed on the salmon and young reindeer that human residents also wanted. Doubtless many other eagles were shot but not reported. We must forget, too, the skyways full of birds left sterile or laying eggs too thin-shelled to support their own weight because of the planeloads of DDT dropped on crops during the post–World War II era of plenty. We must forget that at our bicentennial celebration, the eagle population had reached an all-time low: one thousand breeding pairs. Finally, we must forget the hostile disregard of recent administrations toward threatened and endangered species, nay, toward any species that doesn't feed or clothe or cure us ("Owls die every day," said George Bush's secretary of the interior, Manuel Lujan, of a plan to permit logging in two Oregon counties where the endangered spotted owl builds and hunts and breeds, a plan that would save a mere two hundred jobs for two years).

Once we have temporarily cleared our minds of such associations, we must imagine ourselves into a time when for many, the longing for freedom in Webster's skin-deep sense of the word was as sharp and as compelling as physical hunger, since this new nation, conceived in liberty and justice for all, had drawn hard lines as to who would have it and who would not. The word "freedom" must have had a particularly bitter taste for those whose people had known it before their exportation ("Are the great principles of political freedom and national justice, embodied in the Declaration of Independence, extended to us?" former slave Frederick Douglass asked eighty-six years after the document was signed). It must have had a particularly poignant taste for those who had known it before their removal ("I was born where there were no enclosures and where everything drew a free breath," lamented exiled Yamparika Comanche leader Chief Ten Bears, nine years before the U.S. centennial festivities began. "I want to die there and not within walls"). It must have had a taste one could only imagine for those whose gender had yet to partake of it ("We are assembled to protest against a form of government existing without the consent of the governed," Elizabeth Cady Stanton proclaimed in 1848).

Yet for that elite, powerful minority that had just gained liberation from church and king in 1776, that had just gained the coveted privilege of pledging their allegiance where they chose, the word "freedom" had a heady, sweet taste, like that of fresh fruit to those long at sea. But as many of our great thinkers have argued, freedom *is* indivisible. When it is denied to one, it is denied to all. Not simply because its denial to another establishes a precedent that will eventually reach us, as Thomas Paine cautioned, but because the network of webs that connect members of the living world in patterns that ignore the hard lines we draw between Self and Other and in ways we cannot readily know, means that whatever we give or withhold from others, we give and withhold from ourselves as well. If we deny others their freedoms in an effort to preserve our own, then we become their oppressors, and that role demands more submission and conformity than any flesh-and-blood dictator, since it demands obedience in thought as well as action. Eventually, the sweet taste of freedom for the few becomes the bitter taste of freedom denied to all.

So, in this pristine environment where freedom was a hot and urgent craving for some, a craving so recently satisfied for others that it hadn't yet been dulled by complacency or embittered by denial, we must imagine watching the soaring, gliding eagle, beyond the reach of any other creature, free to follow his whim over unmapped, sparsely peopled regions of the continent, innocent of bounties, cages, and imbalanced competition. The type of freedom that Nature's God intended for us all. The type of freedom worth striving for.

December 31 it is twenty degrees and just beginning to snow. After I visit my father, I walk the three blocks to the riverfront. This is my final look at the Mississippi for at least a few months, since I must return to my riverless Nebraska home. I can't distinguish eagles in the far trees on the Illinois side, but it doesn't matter. I am drawn to the river as much for the sight of open, flowing waters in the midst of a frozen landscape as I am for a glimpse of eagles.

I question the wisdom of keeping the same symbol for more than two hundred years. Last summer I sat on a bench across from the eagle cage at the Children's Zoo in Lincoln where two bedraggled eagles—one, missing a wing—leapt and waited. Each passing parent called the children's attention to the great birds. "Look! Our national symbol." But the birds drew little *genuine* interest: no one lingered until they heard the birds screech or saw them spread or preen their wings. My own children waited at the seal pool until I was finished watching eagles and patrons.

Jung believed that archetypal symbols possess a dual or bipolar nature and are capable of producing diametrically opposed results. Consequently, he advocated a type of therapy in which the analyst "amplified" a symbol by learning all he or she could of its source and meaning through archeology, religion, literature, mythology, art, history, and the dreamer's personal associations. Once the symbol was brought to light, its negative qualities could be weakened and its positive ones strengthened. We, too, can amplify our individual and shared symbols by learning all we can of them from books, direct observation, and other people. Then we will see the eagle as more than just another illustration in the field guide or design on the Great Seal. Then we will restore to this too familiar symbol its full range of meaning and evocative powers. Then we will carry within us the ring of his screech and the image of his wings eclipsing the sun.

But also, a slight revision of a symbol is enough to reawaken us to its power and meaning. Before we can beckon eagles, we must prepare a place where they may gather. Perhaps we should stitch or carve or emblazon a representation of a place where eagles gather on every coin and seal and Boy Scout medal, on every flagpole and military person's shoulder. I do not mean some far northern region in summer where food is abundant and human traffic scarce, but here where bridges rise, pesticides leech, and another highway uproots trees. A place of flowing openness created by bridge supports, rock dams, or rapids. A place of sustenance in the midst of seasonal barrenness. A place where what lives in the depths sometimes swims near the surface where it may be hooked and lifted. A place where what is pulled from dark, watery depths wriggles and glistens in air and light before becoming feathered and taloned.

Spring 1992, December 1993

# STILL CENTER

*How long may we have gazed on a particular scenery and think that we have seen and known it, when at length, some bird or quadruped comes into possession of it before our eyes, and imparts to it a wholly new character?*
HENRY DAVID THOREAU, *Journal*, August 14, 1859

The north edge of the field is bordered by cottonwoods whose heart-shaped leaves shimmer like water. A hawk wheels overhead before disappearing into rippling leaves. Long wands of purple loosestrife sway in the breeze, their delicate petals fluttering. A white moth somersaults midair. A red-winged blackbird perches on the utility pole, swoops into the adjacent pasture, where heavy cattle lumber and chew. Widely spaced clouds drag their shadows across the land.

I step over a sagging barbed wire fence, driving a pair of cursing blue jays from a chokecherry bush. When I set my foot in the long, crackling grasses of the meadow, a plague of grasshoppers explodes in all directions. Once completely over the fence, I pause. I am the stillest living organism in a field of constant motion.

Then I see it: a lean, motionless vertical on the edge of the pond near the back of the pasture. Two horizontal eruptions—a long bill, a brief tail—inform me that this is not a post, a dead sapling, or a particularly thick cattail I am watching. I move closer, hoping that the shimmering, swaying, circling, darting, drifting surroundings will camouflage my slow approach. Imagination fed by field guides and glossy photographs in birding magazines flesh out the details I can't yet see: a black-striped white head, a black-speckled ridge down the front of the long white throat, a gray, hairlike fan over the breast, cinnamon feathers at the top of each leg and spotting the front of each wing, storm-blue wings and back, a golden iris.

I draw as close as I dare, crouch down, and wait. I want to shoo the gnats swarming about my eyes and mouth. I want to rub my bare, weed-stung legs. I want to stretch the cramping muscles in my thighs and lower abdomen. For a moment, I lose my composure and laugh at the idea of a skittish bird like me stalking a master stalker, the great blue heron.

But this is not the first time the great blue has challenged my composure. Despite evidence to the contrary, I persist in believing that this bird is found only in pristine, unmapped regions of the continent. Indeed, at one time, that was her habitat. As recently as 1926, Arthur Cleveland Bent noted that her "native solitudes [are] far from the haunts of man . . . on some far distant point that breaks the shore line of a wilderness lake . . . background of somber forest." Yet in 1987, urban naturalist Steven D. Garber pointed out that several types of herons feed in areas "where previously only the boldest of bird species dared venture." I should not have been surprised, then, to discover a great blue hunting the dirty, shallow waters of the Salt Creek in the transitional part of Lincoln, where cornfields and mega-supermarkets are next-door neighbors. Yet I was. I stood on the concrete bridge with cars and semis whizzing past, so absorbed in the tall bird's tread ("so carefully does he place his foot on the moist ground," John James Audubon writes, "cautiously suspending it for a while at each step of his progress") that I no longer noticed the roar of engines, the stench of burnt fuel, the unnerving dip the bridge made each time a semi rumbled past.

Once, I glimpsed a great blue in flight as I drove across Nebraska on Interstate 80. At first, the bird's sheer size and the nearby Platte River led me to believe it was a sandhill crane I was watching. Yet this was not the balanced flight of the crane. Instead of extending her neck and legs as cranes do, the lanky creature before me pulled her long neck into an easy U and dangled her bent legs behind.

Thoreau once scared three great blue herons into flight—whether accidentally or intentionally, I cannot determine. In the unpolished prose of his

April 19, 1852, journal entry, he captured the birds' movements perfectly: "It was a grand sight to see them rise, so slowly and stately, so long and limber, with an undulating motion from head to foot, undulating also their large wings, undulating in two directions, and looking warily about them. With this graceful, limber, undulating motion they arose, as if so they got under way, their two legs trailing parallel far behind like an unearthly residuum to be left far behind." Thoreau wasn't just watching flight patterns. Indeed, he was witnessing the great blue heron's ability to possess and transform the landscape. "They are large," Thoreau continued, "like the birds of Syrian lands, and seemed to oppress the earth, and hush the hillside to silence, as they winged their way over it, looking back toward us."

For me, it was neither the hunting nor the airborne bird that imparted to the landscape "a wholly new character," but the great blue standing stock-still save for gray breast plumes ruffling in the breeze. As I sat on my heels gazing through my binoculars into the heron's black pupil and yellow nimbus—into the landscape's still center—I was no longer in a pasture whose wild growth and motion distracted me from what I really wanted to see. Rather, I was in a pasture where motion was but a necessary pulse beat. The great blue heron had not only "hushed the hillside to silence," it had silenced me as well.

September 1992

# INTERIORS

▰▰▰▰▰▰▰▰▰▰▰▰

*If the Reason be stimulated to more earnest vision, outlines and
surfaces become transparent, and are no longer seen; causes and spirits
are seen through them. The solid seeming block of matter has been
pervaded and dissolved by a thought.*
RALPH WALDO EMERSON, *Nature*


*It will be objected that the book deals too much with mere appearances,
with the surfaces of things, and fails to engage and reveal the patterns
of unifying relations which form the true underlying reality of
existence. Here I must confess that I know nothing whatever about true
underlying reality, having never met any. There are people who say they
have, I know, but they've been luckier than I.*

*For my own part I am pleased enough with surfaces—in fact, they
alone seem to me to be of much importance. . . . What else is there?
What else do we need?*
EDWARD ABBEY, Introduction to *Desert Solitaire*


*M*any winter days, I pause at Salem Creek to watch for beavers and to
listen to brittle cattail stalks rustling in the wind. Most days, I find
nothing but neutral surfaces: gray, wrinkled water; gray-bottomed sky; ragged,
brown earth. Most winter days, it is too cold to wait for something to break. But
one warm and windless January afternoon, I arrived at the creek just in time to
see a ripple ride the surface between the bank and a heap of brush.

It wasn't a muskrat ripple. Those start from a smaller source and fade to
nothing faster. I guessed a beaver had made this ripple. He was probably already paddling up one of the creek-bed tunnels leading to his lodge or was still
submerged (beavers can swim a good half mile before coming up for air).

When I was a child, Bazooka bubble gum offered glasses that endowed the
wearer with X-ray vision. The advertisement featured the shocked, bespec-

tacled face of a little boy who was seeing through his flesh to the bare bones of his own outstretched hands. I saved wrappers toward the day when those glasses would be mine and I, too, could see through sealed envelopes, gift-wrapped boxes, shirts and pants, walls and skin. But pieces of Bazooka bubble gum were few and far between, and eventually I abandoned my goal. If I had those glasses now, I could verify or refute the diagram of the inner chambers of the beaver's lodge in my field guide: the feeding platform a few inches above the water level, the sleeping platform a few inches above that, plunge holes burrowing through the mud foundation of the nest and opening into water. But my vision is limited to outlines and surfaces—gray water, a heap of peeled sticks, and too solid flesh.

I may not be able to see beavers, but I know they are there—or have been. The woody margin along the top of the bank that parts the creek bed from the field beyond is dotted with cottonwood and oak sapling stumps bearing the distinctive, pointed beaver signature. When I find a tree stripped of bark higher than my knees, I remember that beavers can be four feet long, a quarter of which is tail. Sawdust and chips skirt the base of each stump. Some of the chips open like accordions or paper dolls: work that is of a piece.

Diagonal paths where the ground is worn bare or the weeds flat are the slides down which the beaver drags branches and reeds to his nest and cache. An oak sapling is lodged between a sturdy bush and the trunk of a white ash at the top of the slide. I untangle the branch and shove it down the slide. Then I edge down the bank.

To my left is a soggy stand of cattails. Separating me from the beaver dam on my right is a fallen tree. It is smooth and tan as old bones. It will be of little use to the beaver—all the smaller branches with which he could build are gone. Neither will the trunk feed him since it is not wood he eats but the layer of tissue between the bark and the wood. As I make my way to the water's edge, I find them: beaver tracks. Fine, fingered forepaws; wide, webbed hind feet.

Once I hiked with a naturalist who told me everything she knew about the Salem Creek beavers. She believed it is a bachelor beaver working this bend in the stream and he appears to have vacated his lodge. The naturalist is not certain where he lives now, but she is certain he is near. He has two good caches—one by the lodge, one further upstream—and just recently he knocked down part of his dam because the water was stagnating.

I wonder if the lodge is still inhabited, but because the beaver is so discreet, more finely trained eyes than mine have missed his primarily nocturnal comings and goings. I study the surfaces for clues. The lodge juts from the bank like a peninsula, water on three sides. I search for evidence of mud-plastered walls on this pile of peeled sticks but find none. I read that in the autumn, beavers dredge creek-bottom mud, carry it in their forepaws or between their chin and forepaws and pile it on the sticks. This outer coating of earth is "smoothed as if plastered with a trowel," according to John James Audubon, though never, says Ernest Thompson Seton, does the beaver apply it with his tail. Not only does this stuccoed surface insulate the beavers from the cold, but it strengthens the walls so that coyotes—and in a wilder time, bears, wolves, and wolverines—cannot break in.

But beavers never plaster their roofs. It may be too awkward for them to transport mud to the very top, or they may be foresighted enough to leave the tops open for ventilation. At any rate, chinks remain between the poles. For this reason, a snow-covered lodge can never blend into the winter landscape because the snow is partly or entirely melted at the highest point, says A. Radclyffe Dugmore in *The Romance of the Beaver*. On extremely cold days, a thin vapor rises from the place where the flue would normally be situated. A dead giveaway to a sharp-eyed trapper.

In *World of the Beaver*, Leonard Lee Rue III says that people so pestered European beavers that they stopped building their conspicuous dams and lodges and reverted to bank dens, living like muskrats. Some American beavers have done the same. On the opposite bank, just a few feet above the water level and not far from the cache, lies a hole, less than a foot wide. Perhaps the beaver has taken up residence there. I try to imagine myself into that earnest state of mind that Emerson assures will pervade and dissolve outlines and surfaces. But the bank does not yield. If I could see past the surface, what would I find? A sleeping beaver? A muskrat? A pile of bones, feathers, fur, and teeth? Root hairs and packed dirt? I study the lodge. I see no waves of warm air rising. Even this loosely thatched affair is solid to my eye. I wish the intensity of my gaze could burn a peephole in the wall. First, curls of smoke. Then, a brief flame. Then, ashes and full exposure.

Salem Creek is full of surfaces that I can penetrate. Red-brown scales on the oak sapling I pushed down the slide seal miniature green leaves from moisture loss and cold. If I peel the scales, I can preview spring, though the leaves I expose in January will not survive until the spring. Near the water's edge, I knock on the trunk of the fallen, hollow tree and peer into the hole. Whose sleep am I disturbing? Beetles? A day-sluggish opossum? A barn owl? A ball of honeybees?

The cattail seedheads look like armchairs spilling their stuffing. When I shake some stalks, clouds of seeds and seed hairs ride the breeze. But when

I shake others, nothing is lost because the seeds and hairs are bound by the silk of the cattail moth, whose larvae sleep and feed near the flower's rachis, as close to the core as they can get. To see the larvae now would mean destroying their well-bound bundle of food and insulation. But if I return at the right spring moment, I will see the moths break the surface of the cocoon and rest on the edge of last year's flower, their new, yellow-brown wings just unfurled. If I arrive a minute too late, I will find them flitting above the cattail stand like a mind alive with small ideas.

But these are not the surfaces I want to penetrate. I want to see through water, bank, and lodge so I may determine for myself what is true about the beaver and what is not. Baker writes that the beaver combs his pellage with the split and serrated second claw on each hind foot. I have to see this to believe it. R. G. Beidleman claims that beavers are slow swimmers, but Audubon says they swim "fast and well, but with nothing like the speed of the otter." I must see the beaver swim for myself if I am to know which expert is correct.

The surfaces that conceal the beaver prevent me from determining if I am a patient, silent, still, and transparent observer. While I have successfully stalked white-tailed deer, red foxes, and great blue herons, it is undercover game that vexes me more. If I could peel away all that obscures, I could creep close enough to rest my hand on the beaver's back while he works.

The surfaces that conceal keep me from knowing if my creek is wild enough for the beaver to call it home or if he has moved on to wilder waters. "As I came home through the woods . . . I caught a glimpse of a woodchuck stealing across my path," says Thoreau, "and felt a strange thrill of savage delight, and was strongly tempted to seize and devour him raw; not that I was hungry then, except for that wildness which he represented." The beaver is my woodchuck, my symbol of pure wildness, though I admit that prairie orchids, dung beetles, and sandhill cranes are rarer, more arresting, or more elegant. I have only seen beavers out of context: dirty and lethargic in cement-floored zoo cages, seedy and frozen in museum display cases. These will not suffice. I want to find the beaver at home in his natural element. If that place is Salem Creek, then my creek is not only wild enough for the beaver but it is wild enough to be an antidote for the too long stretches of time I spend thinking like a city—woefully forgetful that the earth is my beginning and my end, that animals are my kin.

Dissolving surfaces isn't the only way in. One can look through ice for bubbles to determine the underwater whereabouts of the beaver and perhaps see his form passing like shadow. Rollin H. Baker, who writes about Michigan beavers, suggests putting one's ear to the lodge roof or, better yet, inserting microphones into the living space and recording the whines, bellows, whistles, and hisses within. Likewise, I've read that some lodge roofs are so open you can peer in and see bright, steady eyes staring back.

Dugmore says he has had an easier time photographing lions and other dangerous beasts than beavers, who not only are "rather shapeless, with inconspicuous legs, [and] no pattern in the way of colouring," but are seldom seen in daylight. Yet he advises photographers to vandalize the dam, which is certain to persuade the beaver to surface and repair it, since he doesn't like to let water escape. Next, the photographer positions her camera on or near the dam, runs a black thread attached to the flash light and shutter over the breach (five inches above the water level to avoid muskrats, says Dugmore), and then waits to catch the beaver as it works.

Audubon reports that when the lodges weren't frozen, prairie Indians opened them and took the beavers. After his "conversion" from Englishman to Apache, but before his conversion from beaver trapper to advocate for the Little People, the curious Archie Belaney (aka Grey Owl) broke a dam, partly drained and then dragged a pond just to capture the mother beaver who had broken the chain on his trap. The Cheyenne used a specially trained dog to antagonize the beaver until it became mad enough to leave the safety of its burrow or tunnel and follow the dog to the surface, where the waiting hunter clubbed the creature to death. Some beaver trappers used the spring-pole, what Grey Owl called a "particularly fiendish contrivance," that yanked the animal uninjured from the water and left him hanging for days until he finally died of thirst and exhaustion.

Some observers gain admittance not by seeing past or by destroying the surfaces and what lies within, but by moving through. While pursued by Blackfoot Indians in 1809, John Colter dove into the water and entered a lodge. Supposedly it did not occur to his pursuers to look for him there, and so he was saved. In *The Cheyenne Indians*, George Bird Grinnell tells about three Cheyenne girls who were sent to the river to fetch water for their mothers. They decided to take a swim before returning and hung their clothes on a tree that had fallen into the water. Beneath the tree, they discovered an opening in the bank. They dove into the water, and as they were swimming up the tunnel, something large and soft passed them, moving in the opposite direction. The girls continued through the tunnel until they saw light ahead—the lodge—which they entered. But they were too unnerved to return the way they'd come, so they burst through the roof into a patch of wild roses, thorny protection against any who tried to enter from above.

Rue attempted to enter a bank lodge built twenty-five feet from the Ottawa River. The tunnels leading from the river to the lodge were half filled with water, their entrances exposed by drought. Rue found one that was large enough—twenty-two inches in diameter—for him to enter. Twelve feet in, he found himself in total darkness and facing a bend in the tunnel. Moreover, as the passageway was becoming smaller, the water level was rising so that Rue had to raise his mouth to the roof in order to breathe. By the time he was eighteen feet in, he could no longer get air. Just ahead, he felt an enlargement in the tunnel and reasoned that there he could turn around by somersaulting. Instead, he got stuck. "When I was completely upside down, I became wedged between the floor and ceiling, and there I stayed," said Rue. "The only thought that flashed through my mind was, "My God, what a place to get it." But it wasn't the end. He finally unwedged himself and backed out. "I often wondered later just what I would have done if I had made it into the lodge only to be greeted by a family of angry beavers ready to protect their home. Perhaps it is just as well that I could go no further."

Most days, I'd back out fast, too. But on my braver days, I might take my chances.

Rue's passage might have been easier had he been invited. Once people did receive such invitations, but it was at a distant time when people were intimate with the earth and those with whom they shared it. It was a time when people believed that beavers were wiser than they.

In *Blackfoot Mythology* [sic], Clark Wissler and D. C. Duvall retell how the Blackfeet received the powerful beaver medicine-bundle. As the story goes, there was a woman who lived on a lakeshore with her husband, a mighty hunter who had acquired many skins, including that of a white buffalo. One day while the man was hunting and the woman was alone, a beaver came out of the water and made love to her. After this happened several times, the woman joined the beaver in his lodge.

When the mighty hunter returned from the hunt, he searched for his wife. All he found were her tracks leading to the lake. When he realized what had happened, he returned home and waited patiently. Four days later his wife returned, heavy with child. After the beaver-child was born, the woman showed him to her husband. The hunter played with his stepson and in time became quite attached to him.

The old, all-knowing beaver was touched by the hunter's kindness toward the beaver-child and decided to give his powerful medicine-songs to the man in exchange for bird and animal skins. When the woman again went to the lake, the beaver instructed her to send her husband to the lodge, where he should do whatever the beaver asked of him in exchange for the songs. It was done. The beaver sang a song and the man paid with a skin, until finally the beaver possessed all the animal skins and the man possessed a bundle full of songs.

In Grinnell's retelling of another Blackfeet legend, an old white beaver invited Api-kunni, a poor man unsuccessful in love and war, to spend the winter in the beaver lodge as his apprentice. Api-kunni agreed. When spring came, he left with two gifts from the beaver: a long aspen stick and a bag of medicine. He easily killed a warrior with the beaver stick. Because of his battle victory and the bag of power, he won the woman he had long desired. Finally, the chief bestowed his lodge, his wives, his servants, and his people upon Api-kunni. Chief Api-kunni had yet one more gift from the beaver: a seed. From it grew tobacco, the most sacred crop of the Blackfeet. "Many strange things were taught this man by the beaver," Grinnell concludes, "which were handed down and are followed till to-day."

So, I press my ear to the wall. I swim long, winding, narrowing tunnels. I pour myself mudlike through the chinks. I save a shoeboxful of bubble gum wrappers. I wait for invitations. Still, all my efforts are like BBs sprayed against bulletproof glass: they don't even dent the surface, much less reveal what lies on the other side.

I have never been at the creek so early in the morning or on such a cold day. The sky is cloudless and far away. But it is not mere backdrop against which clouds and stars and flying machines come and go. The Canada geese that overwinter on a pond near here fly so low I can hear the whir of their wings, I can see their eyes, I can almost leap and touch their breasts. They are in the sky.

The dam is whole again and holds the creek in place. Today, the water is so clear it has no surface. My eyes drag the depths, over clamshells, moss-furred stones, and through runnels, dappled black-and-green streams within the stream. But on turbulent spring days, the creek is all surface: a cheap mirror waving a cloud, budding branches, a crow, my own undulating face. Soon the creek will be frozen, revealing nothing, reflecting nothing. I wish all surfaces were as inconstant as that of water.

Leonardo da Vinci says that water has no surface to see, because a surface is nothing but the shared boundary of two bodies that are not continuous and the surface does not form part of either body. Philosopher Avrum Stroll explains that for Leonardo, surfaces are abstract bodies, and abstract bodies occupy no place in space. Thus, the surface of the water is neither part of the water nor part of the air, and neither do any other bodies come between them. Since this common boundary or interface is invisible and substanceless, nothing of matter separates me from what the depths hold.

Physicist G. A. Somarjai says the surface is the last layer of an object before one moves into a different sort of medium. In other words, the surface is the creek's outermost layer of atoms, assuming there is nothing thinner than that. Like Leonardo's surface, Somarjai's is invisible to the naked eye, but with a powerful lens, I could see the creek's finest, farthest edge. Thus the surface of the creek, that place where leaves drift, bubbles break, Jesus bugs walk, and reflections beckon, is not separate from the creek. Nothing parts me from the depths but the depths themselves.

When Emerson said that stimulated Reason and earnest vision could penetrate and dissolve outlines, he was speaking of surfaces similar to and different from those of which Leonardo and Somarjai spoke. According to Emerson, the Universe is composed of Nature and Soul. In the common sense of the word, Nature refers to "essences unchanged by man; space, the air, the river, the leaf." But in the philosophical sense of the word, Nature is everything, "both nature and art, all other men and my own body." Nature is everything that is not Soul, that is NOT ME. That is, sky begins where I end. But if my own body is part of Nature and my soul is not, then a fine, interior surface separates me from NOT ME. If that surface is penetrable—whether it is composed of atoms and the spaces between those atoms or it is a stratum of nothingness—it should be penetrable from either side. From which direction shall I aim my dive? Upward through sky? Downward through layers of cooling, darkening water? Or should I turn my attention inward, penetrating my own epidermis, my own cornea, my own cortex?

To my right, the cache extends from the bank. A particularly long, barkless branch rises like a flagpole. I look from the thing to its reflection. I begin at the trembling tip and follow it to the trembling lodge. None of this is solid, but wavering like the nature of matter itself. Is this mass of waves more penetrable than the immovable mass I usually see?

The reflection of the burrow in the bank provides a quivering doorway to the watery realm. Fairy-tale children often fell into wells, falling beyond the surface, beyond the threshold of waking awareness into a world of depths and dreams where they discovered their own latent abilities to make the magic that would save them from the water nixie hot on their heels and make them wiser people when they returned to the surface. When shamans returned from their journeys down and out, they brought knowledge that would heal others as well as themselves. I don't hope for as much. I only hope to take the plunge.

I am lulled by the creek in motion. When bubbles break the surface, I am startled even though I know it is not a beaver or even a muskrat but decaying fish or weeds releasing gas. I wait so long that should I have occasion to lift my binoculars, my frozen fingers would be too stiff to work the focus ring.

Within arm's reach stands a cottonwood. Less than a week ago, the trunk was whole and bark-covered, but now it resembles a thick-middled hourglass. I examine a wood chip. It is as long as my thumb, half as thick, and forms a lazy, splintered C. Rue says a beaver gnaws one end of a cut and then the other until he can tear the piece free. The upper incisors do most of the actual cutting, the lowers remain stationary. Rue is right. Five wide terraces score one end of the chip; closer, narrower ones score the other. While beavers are not the only animals that eat cottonwood bark (Custer kept his horses alive one prairie winter on such fare—a trick he learned from the Lakota), no other animals peel away the surface in quite this manner.

I gather chips until my hands are full. They smell fragrant, wild, new. Some of the chips are divided into V's as if the beaver attempted to tear them free before they were ready and then had to nibble further to work the pieces loose. Some of the chips I hold are longer than my longest finger; others are half the length of my shortest finger, since as the beaver gnaws through the layers toward the center, the pieces become smaller.

Atop the bank stands a gnarled, twiggy tree, stripped of its bark in an oval patch twice the width and length of my hand. This is a "blaze," a place where the beaver has tested the bark and found it wanting. This is a place where the beaver has seen the depths revealed in the surface.

I scan the landscape, blazing surfaces as I go. I cannot see the beaver sleeping within the hill or lodge, but I can hold freshly shaved cottonwood chips in the palm of my hand. I cannot see an amphibianlike mammal stroking and gliding through water, but I can trace webbed footprints in the mud with my fingers. I cannot see the larvae burrowed deeply in the cattail seedhead, but I can see that the seeds and fluff are finely bound with strands of silk. I cannot rest my hand on the beaver's flank, but I know I stalk well enough to dissolve my own surfaces and become just another vertical in the frozen landscape, dissolving the surface Emerson draws between me and the NOT ME of Nature. I cannot see my symbol of wildness rise to the top and blink, but I know this creek is wild enough to dissolve the glass and concrete walls of city mind because all winter I've been buying tickets to a show whose curtain never rises.

I cannot dissolve or break or dive past a surface to seize what lies hidden within: it must break of its own accord. Sometimes what lies within erupts like fear or passion or the sudden flush of a night bird or a roiling, rising swarm of bees. Sometimes it nudges gently like a hunch, a budding idea, or the easy pressure of new leaves against winter scales. But mostly, it pours forth from every pore, generously and unceasingly. Now you see, and now you see even more.

February 1992

# FIELD GUIDE
⌐◢◣◢◣◢◣◢◣◢◣◢◣◢◣⌐

*R*idge Boulevard ends at the edge of a soybean field. To the west are re-mains of an abandoned farm; to the east are costly, ostentatious houses, so recently built that the new grass is patchy and all the trees are saplings. On either side of the new street, gold HOME Real Estate signs mark each lot. They are brighter than the weedy yellow composites.

I walk to this jagged edge each day not to watch workers hammering raw mock-Tudor and Cape Cod frames or laying gas pipelines, but to gaze miles into the distance where the sky meets a far line of cultivated fields and treetops. I come to observe how mugwort, lamb's quarters, ragweed, and bull thistles have reclaimed the broken ground. And, I come for the birds. Here, sharp-edged swallows move freely between fields and suburban backyards. Crows swagger in the bean field. Red-winged blackbirds bubble their bright notes from fence posts. In the far distance where cemetery and bean field meet, a red-tailed hawk wheels.

Last week, after a late-afternoon rain, I returned to the Edge. The swallows were diving so close they startled me. Mourning doves were picking gravel. Legions of invisible sparrows chirped in the long grass. Suddenly, I heard an unfamiliar call: rasping notes with clean spaces between. I looked in the direction of the call, but all I saw were fast-moving cumulus clouds. The calls stopped as two brown-and-white birds landed in the vacant lot before me. They dashed and paused, dashed and paused. One bird jumped on the back of the other, surveyed the field, then jumped off. I crept through the mud after them. They were not timid, and I could draw within twenty feet of them before they darted to put more space between us.

My walk home was less than a mile but seemed farther, since I was trying to retain details of the birds' form and plumage: beak longer and sharper than a robin's, two light stripes along the side of the head, a brown back, a lighter belly (had there been flecks or stripes or some other pattern?), a white-edged tail, a flash of rust—though I cannot say if I saw it on the bird or in the background.

I have used field guides only to flesh out details about birds that other people have identified for me—my first purple finch, my first whippoorwill. Then I was struck by the differences between the guidebook model and the real thing, since plumage in the field is seldom as bright or as delineated as the sketched form; subjects are never as still, the light rarely as good, nor do the bird calls or songs match the descriptions ("a kong-ka-ree, 4–9/min." makes sense only because I already know the song of the red-winged blackbird). The authors of field guides claim their books are not just for veteran birdwatchers, yet these experts seem to have forgotten how one bird can look and sound so much like the next to an untrained eye and ear.

Because of my mystery bird's long legs and beak, its high body and preference for walking over flying, I guessed it might be a shorebird. The characteristic stance of the spotted sandpiper, for instance, is "with body tilted forward, head held low." But this common sandpiper flocked near fresh water. Other than a very slim and choked farm creek that the developers would soon bottom with cement, I knew of no near water—fresh or otherwise.

If my unknown was a perching bird, my search would be limited to the last 137 pages (excluding bibliography and index) of Robbins, Bruun, Zim, and Singer's *Birds of North America*. But this did not mean 137 distinctly different species. Crowded on one page, I found fifteen surprisingly similar though different species of olive or yellow immature female fall warblers without wing bars. On the next page, I found eighteen olive or yellow immature female fall warblers with wing bars and tail spots. More variations on one theme than I had imagined possible. "Immatures, especially females, require careful study," the field guide cautioned.

Like my nameless bird, the female lark bunting had the same white and brown coloring, a white stripe on the side of the head (had I seen one or two?), and was often observed picking seeds on or near the ground in shortgrass prairie. Yet the only remaining prairie in eastern Nebraska exists in small preserves maintained by the university or in ragged strips along abandoned railroad tracks, and it is tallgrass. I would have to drive half a day to reach the blue grama and buffalo grass home of the lark bunting.

Pipit seemed another likely answer to my riddle, because both the water pipit and Sprague's pipit are at home in the northern Plains. The description of the latter matched what I had seen: "Unlike Water Pipit, this bird is hard to see. On the ground it remains hidden in tall grasses; when flushed, it flies for a few hundred feet, then drops into heavy cover again." Yet what kept me from pronouncing my bird a pipit was the description of the call as a "weird hissing." I had heard my bird deliver only a single tone, robust, broken, and unmelodious. Once, I thought I heard it end in a trill.

If not a pipit perhaps a horned lark. This little bird also had a white belly, a brown back, and a black collar. But the lark had a yellow face; it was white head stripes I had seen. Neither did my mystery bird sport horns, though this did not mean my bird was not a horned lark. The field-wise John James Audubon hadn't recognized the immature bald eagle as such because it lacked the distinctive white head feathers, and so he named his "new" species the Washington eagle. Likewise, I may have been observing the smooth head and pale face of an immature horned lark.

But what was happening to me? I *knew* what a horned lark looked like. When I was twelve or thirteen, my mother raised an orphaned horned lark to maturity and then released it in the wilds north of Burlington. I can still remember Melody's delicate feet and bill, her feathered tufts and sweet song. Yet the bird I had been watching at the Edge was neither delicate nor melodious. An hour with the field guide left me doubting what I had thought I knew with certainty. The right name was even further away. It was time to close the book.

A name distinguishes the nameless-though-significant from less significant background. Not just another pink flowering forb but a lady's thumb, for instance. Names are also economical: instead of saying I picked a branched stem covered with small daisylike flowers (flat yellow centers circled by two or three sets of white rays, the entire flower half an inch across) and widely varying leaves (the lower ones, long and toothed ovals; the upper ones, smooth-edged lances), I could communicate the same cluster of information by saying I had picked a daisy fleabane.

Equally important is that the act of bestowing a name imparts the grand opportunity "to seal finally every object and every event with a sound and thereby at the same time take possession of it," as Friedrich Nietzsche wrote. If I can name the bird, it is mine. Nietzsche's choice of the verb "to seal" is no accident. As soon as one chooses and bestows a name on another, one's perception of the other is shut and sealed to revision except in rare instances. Once you've determined that the tree whose brown bark loosens and curls like old paint and whose dry crushed leaves smell of cinnamon is a sycamore, you probably won't plan a closer, second encounter to note that under the curling outer bark is a white-green layer with a chartreuse primer coat beneath it or that the aroma of the dry leaves is muskier and milder than cinnamon or any other spice you can name. Once you have enough evidence to match the object to its given name, there's no reason to keep looking—unless you just happen to love sycamores. The stubborn finality of a name and the imbalance of power it implies so divides and distances the namer and the named that they can never become intimate in the fullest sense of the word.

Philosopher Susanne K. Langer writes that "primitive" peoples often did remain intimate with what they had named because they saw names as "physical proxies for their bearers." They knew that to call an object by an inappropriate name was to confound its very nature. Since "the little, transient, invisible breath that constituted a spoken word" was the most "concentrated point of sheer meaning," a name carried "more definition and momentous import than any permanent holy object," says Langer. By knowing the name, they could bring forth the object or experience to which that name referred as if from thin air. In the beginning was the name.

But for most of us, the power of a single word to create an entire cosmos is but anthropological hearsay. We live with such a proliferation of words and names that we no longer see how such small units of meaning can connect us with our experiences. In *House Made of Dawn*, Kiowa author N. Scott Momaday observes that the modern white man "has diluted and multiplied the Word, and words have begun to close in on him. He is sated and insensitive; his regard for language—the Word itself—as an instrument of creation has diminished nearly to the point of no return." Consequently, the modern white man will "perish by the Word," Momaday predicts.

The challenge for those of us who have never really experienced the connection between a word and its referent lies not in those rare opportunities in which we are called to bestow a first-time and fitting name for a new country, virus, planet, or human being but in restoring an inherited name to the realm of the sacred, where it is an incantation, a holy utterance, the ultimate creative act.

When I returned to the jagged edge I was full of names. A few moments in the shorebird section of my field guide, and I discovered that my bird was one of the banded plovers, *plovier* being Old French for "rain." It was a "rain bird" I had been observing. Because this plover dramatically feigns injury by extending one wing over her back while beating the other against the ground to distract intruders whenever her nest is threatened, "charade" is the root of her genus name, *Charadirus*. Because of her clamorous, insistent, grating call, *vociferus* is her species name. And the sounds of the rain bird's call provide her common name: killdeer, a name I'd heard dozens of times.

Killdeer. I have only to say the name and I am at the Edge. A hot, stiff wind shakes and bends stems and leaves while I wait for the birds to arrive. Hammering rings across the blank, blue sky. The fields flutter with birds, though not the ones I came to see. I hear thin, well-punctuated ascending rasps that thicken as the distance lessens. Then the birds are there atop a newly broken ridge of earth. I note how closely the living bird matches the sketched form: for the first time I see the red rim about the eye, the splotch of red on the tail that is there even when the wings are closed, the point where the two black neck bands disappear into brown nape feathers. And, too, I note what the field guide does not say: that the bird itself is the streaking, halting, rasping expression of a place where city and country; suburb, farm, and prairie; land and sky; named and unnamed meet.

Summer 1993

# RUSTLINGS

**S**omething is coming undone. White tufts of wool drift toward the earth. Dirty white clumps lie flat and sodden on the pavement, still damp from an early-morning rain. Tufts snagged on cedar needles wave in the breeze. I look for the origin of this summer snow. Not far ahead of me I see furrowed gray bark. Glossy green hearts on stems rittle in the breeze, flashing pale undersides. The crown is broad and open. I face the rising sun and soften my gaze until only gold light and this slow snow remain.

Evidence of the cottonwood's fecundity surrounds me. The breeze tugs seed-bearing hairs from the capsules notching each catkin, those scaly spikes bearing the cottonwood's petalless flowers. Each catkin contains sixty capsules. Each capsule contains dozens of seeds. Each cottonwood tree bears two hundred, three hundred catkins. Maybe more. I will not get lost in calculations, yet if the earth were not so paved, trodden, mowed, and poisoned, it would be nothing but seas of rustling cottonwoods.

I leap to catch a drifting ball of seeds and hairs. I don't feel solid movements like those of a caught fly, buzzing and thumping for ways out. I open my palm. It is there: a wisp of low-riding cloud.

In *The Plant Tribes*, Melvin R. Gilmore says that the cottonwood to be felled for the center pole of the Dakota Sun Dance must be one "the base of whose trunk is not less than two spans [nine inches] in circumference . . . straight to a distance from the ground of about four times the measure of the outstretched arms from hand to hand, where it must be forked." I sit on the ground and lean my back against a cottonwood trunk of sacred dimensions. Cool air streams down the tree's trunk and my spine.

The first cottonwood I have clear memories of was too broad for my arms to span. It grew on the south bank of a creek that ran through my parents' Iowa pasture. Because cottonwood leaf stalks are slightly flattened, they are highly responsive to the slightest movement of the wind. Even on the stillest days, the leaves shimmered and spoke.

One night, strong winds split a main branch from the trunk. The next morning, I found the limb spanning the creek from bank to bank, the leaves fluttering greenly in the breeze, speaking in tongues I could not understand, uttering their last words before they turned stiff and brown. But even then, the wind could move them to speak.

In autumn, yellow leaves and slips of twigs (the latter wedged free by layers of cork cells sealing the wounds of separation) were dragged downstream by the current. Where a twig or seed stuck in the mud, it took root. The following fall, the banks of the creek downstream in the neighboring cow pasture were thick with saplings, tall as my shoulder, rustling with vowels and consonants. A stream of words.

I pull to the side of the gravel road (there is no shoulder), wade through the tall grasses and goldenrod in the ditch, and stop next to a barbed wire fence. These cottonwoods were probably planted as a windbreak, but on this still and searing September day cattle nod in their shade.

The cottonwood is the tree of tender mercies. In this austere land, where most trees must be planted and coaxed, it flourishes, makes shade, mitigates the wind. In this dry land, its roots tap deep water. In this frugal landscape, it remakes itself prodigiously. After immigrating from Virginia to Nebraska, Jim Burden, the protagonist in Willa Cather's *My Ántonia*, observed, "Trees were so rare in that country [Nebraska], they had to make such a hard fight to grow, that we used to feel anxious about them, and visit them as if they were persons. It must have been the scarcity of detail in that tawny landscape that made details so precious." A clump of cottonwoods on a prairie stream, a cottonwood windbreak near a farmhouse, a lone cottonwood on the edge of a pasture were sights for sore eyes.

Legend tells that the leaves of this tree taught people how to live. Gilmore says that when Plains Indians rolled heart-shaped leaves between forefingers and thumbs, they conceived of the design for their conical, open-topped homes. And the cottonwood taught people where to live. In *My Life on the Plains*, George A. Custer wrote that Indians always built their winter villages upon the point of a stream "promising the greatest supply of timber, and the village was strewn with the white branches of the cottonwood entirely stripped of their bark." Grouse, rabbits, squirrels, porcupine, deer, and horses fed on tender cottonwood parts when other forage was scarce in the harsh winters of the Northern Plains. Even Custer fed his horses and mules "long forage" when he went on winter Indian raids.

I gaze upon these trees so long that I lose my will to leave. My feet become rooted. My gray, furrowed limbs reach. As jays leap and land, I tic and shudder. My vision is diffused. I see from every light-catching cell. A breeze stirs and I utter streams of language, too quick and fluid to be parted into words, too quick for my understanding. The sun on my crown is hot. Bunched cattle breathe softly in my shade.

I drive south through farmland. Few verticals break the sameness of the view until I pass a lowland east of the highway, crowded with cottonwoods. I am grateful for their verticals. The few leaves remaining on these trees are mostly on the highest branches. The rest lie in sodden, silent layers on the ground. I am pressed to say what these widely spaced gold leaves remind me of. Daytime stars? An autumn rash? Holes in my logic? Tremoring gold notes above my head?

My tires are the first to cut the snow on the road. I slow as I near the cottonwood by the barbed wire fence. Its thousand singing tongues are still beneath the drifts. The tree's skeleton is not gnarled, arched, or twisted like the hickories and elms I meet in the park. Nor do cottonwood limbs rustle with brown leaves like the white oak. Instead, these limbs are bare, straight, and silent. "You cannot mount a rock and preach to a tree how it shall attain the kingdom of heaven," writes Donald Culross Peattie in *The Flowering Earth*. "It is already closer to it, up there, than you will grow to be."

The catkin I saved from last June has dried and turned back on itself, a snake biting its own tail. I tease clumps of seeds and down from the split capsules. These seeds will not perish on thistle, rock, or sterilized lawn. I lay them in plastic flowerpots filled with potting soil. In time, I will have enough trees to break any winter blast. Enough trees to green-fringe the Platte. Enough trees to sustain a field of deer and grouse or rings upon rings of Indian ponies. Enough words to fill the sky.

It is January. On the other side of the window, everything is frozen and white. At this distance, the sun's light is frail. But on the windowsill, in the warmth and light of my kitchen, it is spring. A pure stand of cottonwoods unfurls new tongues. I exhale warm breezes and listen. It is a newly created world and the trees will teach me to speak. From the beginning.

October 1991

# FIELD OF VISION

$I$ can count on one hand the number of years I have not been on the Mississippi at mayfly time, those few days when the flies come shoreward in droves for a fleeting aerial dance. Yet, of all those cusps between spring and summer, only once—last year—did I really see them, allowing them to hover about me, to land on my hand, where I observed the fine balance achieved by the upward lift of the pincerlike forelegs, the center arch of the ten-segmented abdomen, the backward extension of the tail filaments, V-parted when alive, joined in death. When the dance ended, I collected their delicate corpses and took them home. Under strong light, I examined the veins and cross veins on their translucent wings and the honeycombed lenses of their eyes that, when viewed from the side, are more of a head than the actual head.

It was my brother's June wedding that took me home to Iowa. The reception was held at the Memorial Auditorium, a mammoth green WPA structure just feet from the cemented riverbank. The bride directed the photographer and the groom toward a twitching maple, its limbs weighted with dull blossoms, its trunk shagged with rustling fur. The pictures would be taken there, with the green span of McArthur Bridge to the north, the wide gray river in the background, and the sun-filled floodplains of west-central Illinois beyond that. But when they neared the tree, it exploded with hundreds of dun-colored mayflies that clung to my brother's rented tuxedo and the bride's white gown, lighting about their mouths and ears and eyes. The bride batted them with her gloved hands, cursing her own poor timing. Evidently the flies came now as they always did on our stretch of the river. Of course. No nuptial celebrations or riverfront carnivals had ever dissuaded them.

It is the brevity of the Ephemeroptera's winged existence that charms and appalls. It led Dr. Hugh Williamson to observe before the American Philosophical Society in 1802 that this "insect of the hour," the only winged insect that never sees the sun, "might serve for a strong figure in the hands of a peevish philosopher." And, indeed, it has. In "Soliloquy of a Venerable Ephemera Who Had Lived Four Hundred and Twenty Minutes," Ben Franklin's speaker laments that all his earthly labors, his philosophical studies, and political struggles were for naught, since in seven or eight minutes, the sun would drop into the ocean, forever extinguishing itself and all earthly existences.

Peevishness aside, the mayfly is an object lesson in mutability if we only see what is immediately apparent. In its winged stage, this creature has but one purpose: procreation. Behavior and biology are honed toward that end. The alimentary canal, that passage through which food passes, becomes a large air sac, permitting the insect to hover, rising on quick wings, then falling on still ones, rising and falling, nearly defying gravity in its nuptial flight. Into this buoyant, dancing swarm of males enter the larger, heavier females. The insects couple in midair and part, each female to oviposit her two thousand to eight thousand eggs over water before dying, the males to continue swarming until sometime before sunrise when they, too, fall, their soft bodies littering the riverfront, in some spots drifted deep like snow.

In the space of a day, it is done.

If I were to creep up the river one fifty-mile segment per day, I would meet a mayfly hatch at every stop, beginning at the delta, where the mayfly really does emerge in May, and ending at the source at Lake Itasca, where the mayfly arrives in July. At each stop, I would hear them cursed by one of their various names—cisco flies, shad flies, herring flies, dayflies.

In my hometown of Burlington, Iowa, we called them Mormon flies, a reference to that time nearly a century and a half ago when many of the 19,000 residents of Illinois' then largest city, Nauvoo, just thirty miles downstream, packed their belongings and walked the frozen river to Sugar Creek and Richardson's Point west of Montrose, Iowa, where they awaited the spring. Their former leader, Joseph Smith, and his brother Hyrum had been slain in the Carthage jail by a mob of angry "gentiles" in 1844. Early in 1846, the new leader, Brigham Young, received a vision of a promised land in the Great Basin. Crossing the mighty river was the first step there. His disciples swarmed shoreward in hordes . . . legions . . . battalions.

My grandmother complained bitterly about the Mormon flies. Their pellicles, the result of their final molt, made her eyes tear and her nose run. And, they stunk. Thus, another name: stink bugs.

But we also called them river bugs, since they confined themselves to a narrow strip on either side of the river. Five blocks away, only an occasional stray clung to storefront windows or fluttered about a lighted sign. Because of their density along the river, their presence disrupted more than one riverfront carnival, including Steamboat Days in my hometown and the World's Longest Street Fair in Keokuk, Iowa, where my grandparents lived. The flies swarmed about the streetlights and the lights on concession stands and rides. Some years, the bingo games played in a canvas tent for real prizes—rods and reels or TV sets—were moved into the auditorium because the mayflies obstructed vision and hung annoyingly from the lower edges of card tables and folding chairs, like sleeping bats. The next morning, their spent remains were swept to the curb along with flattened snow cone holders, crushed kernels of caramel corn, and torn ticket stubs.

Some river cities attempt retaliation, but no insecticide works. Since mayflies are attracted to lights, some cities simply leave their outside lights off during the hatches. In other cities, street crews sand the bridges and streets, since decomposing mayflies create driving conditions every bit as hazardous as snow. Cars that venture out before the streets have been plowed risk becoming stuck in the wet drifts.

But whether I was sunning on the dock outside my brother's river cabin, awaiting my turn on the Tilt-a-Whirl, or using the night deposit box at Farmers and Merchants Bank and Trust at Third and Jefferson, the mayflies were always in the background, little more than an ephemeral nuisance.

What constitutes background and foreground, figure and field? It is more than mere proximity. If it were simply that, I should have noticed the mayfly to the exclusion of everything else: not only were mayflies underfoot and hovering about my head, but occasionally one would drop down my blouse and bat against my skin until I pulled the cloth loose and shook it free. What led me to twist the focus ring, pulling the mayfly from blurred background to definite object?

Gestalt theorists offer an explanation. They say we simplify the perceptual process by distinguishing "figure," which is central to our awareness, from "ground," that area that surrounds the figure. Ground is the remainder of our perceptual field, which we perceive vaguely if we perceive it at all. It lacks form and definition, appearing insubstantial and quiescent, the color "filmy." Figure, on the other hand, not only possesses greater form, but has denser color, is more compact. Consequently, the figure is what we name first when asked, "What do you see out there?" It appears substantial: solid, impenetrable, defined, and delimited. So insistent is its presence that when our visual contact with the field is broken, the form and detail of the figure persist in memory.

But figure and ground are not fixed categories. Just about every introductory psychology text contains diagrams illustrating the "figure-ground reversal effect," the drawings and the term both creations of the Dane Edgar Rubin. In one drawing, for instance, we are asked to gaze at a square containing a black background and a white interior. What do we see? Two facing profiles or a vase? Focus slides between the two. We see both, but never simultaneously.

It is easily explained. The vase and the silhouettes share a common boundary. But this common boundary lends shape to only one field at a time—whichever we perceive as object at that moment. But since in the case of the illustration, both parts of the field are competing for the shape-giving function of the contour, what we see as figure or ground alternates back and forth at a dizzying speed. Rubin explains that the purpose of his ingenious drawing is to provide the viewer with the opportunity "not only to convince himself that the ground is perceived as shapeless but also to see that a meaning read into a field when it is figure is not read in when the field is seen as ground." When we perceive a vase, the black area is filler. But when we perceive the black space as a tête-à-tête, the white area between is not vase as much as it is a distance to be crossed.

I suspect we see figure because that object is invested with more personal meaning or value than anything else within our field of vision. The Gestaltist would beg to differ. He would say we distinguish figure spontaneously and immediately and that this ability is neither learned nor conscious. In his 1929 *Gestalt Psychology*, Wolfgang Kohler stated that sensory organization "appears as a primary fact which arises from the elementary dynamics of the nervous system." In other words, what we perceive as figure is simply the end product of sensation. A purely mechanical process. Even congenitally blind people differentiate between figure and ground as soon as they become sighted through cataract surgery, according to M. V. Senden's 1932 research. The eye needs no training or experience. Rubin concedes that when given "nonsense figures," subjects do attempt to read meaning into them, making them into something known—"birds, animals, people, flowers, or coffee-cans, crochet hooks, etc., but sometimes more abstract forces, tendencies, directions, and movements" as well. This attempt at meaning making occurs after the eye has already pulled figure from the ground; it is not, however, the determining factor in the selection process.

The Gestaltist is correct. We do possess the innate capacity to differentiate, but I believe it is more than simply mechanical or instinctive. The impulse to differentiate carries a value judgment, and value judgments are derived. There is more to this act of perception than meets the eye.

So what is the starting point? What relegates river, the bridge, the maple tree, the floodplain, the photographer, and the insect swarms to unfocused ground while the bride and the groom are clearly figure? Or why is it that when asked my life story, I perceive the daily ebbs and flows as mere connective tissue between the real figures: the arrivals and departures of loved ones, my losses, my gains, my relocations, and the anniversaries of all these things. More ultimately revealing than the details of my resume is that the last time I felt that guttedness which I know as loneliness was nearly six years ago (I can recall the time and the place) or that despite my surface optimism, my worldview is so clearly apocalyptic that it precludes pension plans, life insurance, and property ownership. Or why is it that after months of walking unvarying city routes and routines I return from a weekend drive through the Nebraska countryside with an eye more teeming with remembered images of mileage signs and billboard ads than of dried streambeds, low groves of flaming sumac, or the steep eroded bluffs on the Iowa side of the Missouri? Occasionally, I would welcome a little figure-ground reversal. But my focus is in need of lubrication: at times such as these it remains unmoved.

Yet just last week, it slid too freely.

In the modern art room at the university gallery, I stand before wide canvases with bold streams and swatches of color. At home, I gaze upon library folio prints of abstract art, the types of work in which untrained eyes such as mine find little evidence of either skill or talent in composition. Yet I am grateful because my eyes find nothing here to fret me with questions about how I value and order the world of the canvas, how I sort stimuli into two piles, figure and field, a hot wash for the former, a cold for the latter. These paintings are field-less, and that is precisely the point. The sole focus is the artist's perception of object, no matter how private or nonrepresentational that interpretation may be. The French painter Georges Braque once said as much of his own composition process: "Without having striven for it, I do in the end change the meaning of objects and give them a pictorial significance which is adequate to their new life." That is the way it is with vision. When we perceive, we judge and order, pulling forth that which has most value, assigning the rest to unseen background. There is no other way.

After days moving through the fieldless world of abstract art, it happens. I am gazing upon a folio reproduction of Mark Rothko's *No. 8,* a simple and famous painting in which the canvas is divided into a top and bottom half with a layer of white between. The bottom half is a vivid block of tangerine with a mustard-yellow border. The top half is a white mass rising from the center bottom—a pastel blue line—which fills two thirds of the upper rectangle. Above and on either side of this burden of ice is yellow. It is the top half that beckons my attention, and for the simplest of reasons: the quality of the white and the yellow pleases me. But then judgment seeps in. I see that the yellow frames the whiteness—and then that the whiteness emerges from the yellow. My focus glides back and forth between these perceptions too fast for me to catch. What kind of dawn is breaking in this upper region, I wonder?

I enter the world of Brueghel. No visual tricks here. Figure is figure and background is background. Flemish painters understood the difference. I turn the big pages of the folio and stop at *The Hunters in the Snow.* In the left foreground, three hunters followed by a pack of hounds trudge through the snow, about to begin their descent of the hill, their backs toward me. I see only a flash of nose and cheek as one hunter turns to address the dogs. Center left, peasants feed a bonfire with straw. In the distance rise craggy mountains. In the valley at the lower right are two ponds' worth of skaters and some incidental traffic along the ponds' perimeters—a horse-drawn cart loaded with wood, a woman carrying kindling on her back, a man attempting to catch a bird in the bush—and beyond, houses and churches. A full but simple canvas. Prominent figure. Busy background. Nothing here to pull me away from the hunters, the real figure. Nothing, that is, until I read what the series commentator, Timothy Foote, says he sees. Of course, his knowledge of the historical context leads me to see present details in greater fullness: "While nature is frozen to a standstill under glacial green skies," Foote writes, "Bruegel's peasants enjoy the one time of year when husbandry is not a burden. Their principal outdoor tasks are hauling firewood or tossing shovelfuls of snow on an occasional chimney fire." I am stopped. I had seen the skies, the people clustering about the fire preparing to singe a pig for a feast, as Foote later explains, and I had seen the people hauling firewood, but that chimney fire is a mystery to me. I search and find it. It is dead center. Flames leap from a cottage chimney. A ladder leans against the side of the house. One person is atop. One is below. Two others cross the nearby footbridge, perhaps to assist. While skaters skate and hunters trudge, the fire, the drama of the canvas, is unseen. I do not like the implications of this.

My blindness to what was most central—literally and figuratively—might not have happened if I could have made my eye innocent when I first approached the painting, if I could have lost my focus and allowed equality to all details. Perhaps then whatever was there could have presented itself.

I test my hypothesis when my son brings me one of his crayoned drawings. I fight focus. I see only a field of swirling colors. Then, they emerge. A gazelle. Larkspurs. A burning bush. Many-portaled cliff dwellings. But my son is chagrined. I haven't seen what is there at all. And he proceeds to identify a long-torsoed horse, weapon-wielding movie heroes, a flaming rocket, and a spotted firehouse dog. Of course. Now I see it. What had emerged from the field was only what I was disposed to see and draw myself.

Vision cannot be made innocent. But by hook or crook, it can be redirected.

Focusing is a dangerous thing. Spend an evening at the depot waiting for a train so late that connections may be missed, but not so late that this is certain. Watch the curve of the track continuously for the beam of light. Once you have boarded, ask yourself: was the moon full? Did clouds drift before it or were the heavens clear, alive with stars? Did quick shadows nip the rim of the yellow circle of lamplight within which you stood or was your vision so tunneled on the one, not-yet stimulus that you saw nothing else?

One of my students, from Seward, Nebraska, teaches me about focusing. He is a hunter and testifies that over the years, his vision has become more refined, his focus more channeled. For instance, in the late autumn when everything in the timber is brown and vertical, his eyes seek the one brown horizontal: the deer. But what of those verticals he has excluded? Just last week, he was hunting not for deer but for wild turkey. His visual range was the trail only, which he scrutinized for turkey tracks and droppings. Once he looked up, and not thirty feet away stood three brown horizontals. But it was not deer he was seeking and, consequently, it was deer he almost missed seeing. This matter of focusing.

My office mate is a watercolorist. She tells me of a trick she knows. When she cannot draw the object—a face, a bowl of fruit, a tree—because she has focused too long and too hard upon it, she shifts her concentration to the space surrounding her object and draws that shared boundary that Rubin exploited in his diagrams. For some reason that my office mate does not understand, drawing from the perspective of the field makes her better able to see and to draw her object.

What kind of vision is possessed by those who see the mayfly not as field but as figure? Surely, an entomologist with an eye for absence and suggestion would find her vision directed not toward the praying mantis, the two-spotted ladybug, the common housefly, or any other genera in her field of study, but toward the mayfly, which is remarkable for what it does not do or have. Certain body parts are conspicuously absent during the adult stage—the mouth and the middle tail, for instance—and the hind and middle legs are so useless that the mayfly can neither walk nor climb. True flies are wingless until they pupate, but mayflies omit this third stage in the customary cycle of egg, larva, pupa, adult. However, in their venerable 1935 work, *The Biology of Mayflies*, James G. Needham, Jay R. Traver, and Yin Chi Hsu note that a hint of these wing structures, "signs of impending transformation," begin to appear at the close of the nymphal stage. With each successive molt, the wing pads become larger, thicker, and darker. As the wings expand—and this is when one needs an eye for suggestion, I believe—they form crumpled, accordionlike folds that can be seen through the transparent sheaths. I should like to see these new wings pressing for release. I should like to see them if I could.

Without an eye for suggestion, entomologists Richard W. Merritt and J. Bruce Wallace would not have returned from their laboratory with electron micrograph photos revealing the bizarre feeding mechanisms of the *Isonychia* nymphs, photos that I photocopied from an old *Scientific American* and studied on my kitchen table. Supposedly, the forelegs of the nymphs of this genus bear thick fringes of bristlelike setae, each of which bears two rows of hairs, one row long, the other row short and hooked. The hooked hairs on one row of legs catch the long hairs on the other, thus forming a snowshoelike structure that strains food particles from the water. Put this in perspective. The length of this creature from tip to tail is nine to seventeen millimeters. This is less than an inch. Maybe, less than a half inch. How long must the leg be, or the seta on that leg, or the hair on the seta of that leg? Moreover, because the nymph has no fighting defenses against predators, its only safety lies in remaining undetected. It is carefully camouflaged. A river nymph clings to stones or weeds, barely visible in the murky water of the Mississippi. Even less apparent is the still water nymph, which digs U-shaped burrows in the pond-bottom ooze. And, when a nymph moves, it darts faster than the eye. When it stops, it stops completely, posed and nearly motionless. Unless one has an eye for suggestion, an eye that can detect the vibration of the respiratory gills, five or six strokes per second with seta-thin pauses between, or the alternating swing of the antennae, the nymph remains unseen, simply part of the field.

Other mayfly experts have an eye for relationships and readily see the parts forming the whole. Applied mayfly biology, it is called. Consider the case that G. F. Edmunds, S. L. Jensen, and L. Berner relate in *Mayflies of North and Central America* (1976). In the 1940s and 1950s increased flow of organic pollution—sewage and agricultural runoff—so enriched Lake Erie that filter-feeding mayflies flourished until the shore was dark with their numbers. As nymphs, they had ingested the added nutrients, emerged, flown to shore, swarmed, and died, their decomposing bodies returning tons of phosphates and nitrates to the land whence it came. While a little may be good, too much is not. The mayflies were overwhelmed by the feast and their numbers plummeted. Before 1953, nymphs had averaged 350 to 400 per square meter. In some places, their numbers reached 9,000. In 1957, however, they averaged 37 per square meter. In 1962, there were none. Edmunds, Jensen, and Berner concluded that if the lake was to be recovered, humans would have to halt the nutrient flow themselves, since the mayflies were no longer there to harvest and transport it back to the land. For those such as the ecologist, whose vision is trained to see not just the parts but the links between the parts, there is no contest: so inextricably linked are they that river, land, and fly together compose the figure.

The first real mayfly experts were the most practical of entomologists: they were anglers. These people had an eye not only for relationships but for transitions as well. They discovered that by using bait that simulated their prey's seasonal food supply, they could increase their catch. Thus, the art of constructing artificial flies—wet flies, resembling the nymphal and just-emergent stages of the mayfly's life, and dry flies, resembling the winged adult stage.

Supposedly the first known flytier was a Macedonian trout fisher who, before throwing out his hook two thousand years ago, wrapped it in wool and lashed a couple of yellow feathers to the sides for wings. Fifteen centuries later, Dame Julianna Berners, or Barnes, as it is sometimes spelled, composed a curious little work called "The Treatyse of Fysshynge with an Angle." Among other matters, Berners instructed her readers in designing the appropriate lures for each month, March through August. As close as I can tell, it is the "maure fly," the Moorish fly—a type of *Ephemera*, according to Thomas Satchell's 1883 glossary of the text—that is the mayfly. It appears in June and, according to Dame Julianna, its form is best imitated by using "the body of doske wull the wynges of the blackest mayle of the wylde drake." A few centuries later, the world's greatest fisher, Izaak Walton, provided directions for constructing may-fly lures in *The Compleat Angler*, which first appeared in 1653: "First for a May-flie, you may make his body with greenish coloured crewel." Today the art is technical and scientific. Flytiers read manuals and attend weekend-long work-shops. Supplies are specially ordered. Quills, feathers, furs, and fibers are used to represent different species at different stages in their life cycle. Attention to detail is meticulous, right down to the silk threads that reproduce the segmen-tation of the abdomen. So keenly aware of the Ephemeroptera life cycle are these fishers that they have even created a prostrate fly that floats on the water surface like the "spent" female that has just oviposited and expired.

But the real art is found not in the likeness between the living fly and the effigy; it lies in the fisher's sense of timing. To be able to perceive the exact mo-ment when the emerging subimago—the winged creature that has yet to molt for a final time—has become an emerged subimago, a change that occurs in a moment, and to respond accordingly demands the refined vision of one who perceives transitions.

Vision is not simply the end product of sensation, as some would have it. Rather, it is the beginning of interpretation. "Thinking," C. S. Peirce tells us, "begins with perception." Thus, perception can never be a neutral act. From our first blink, our vision is opinionated. Not only can the eye never again be made innocent, but it never was in the first place.

E. M. Forster writes of the difficulty, the impossibility of looking cleanly and innocently in his essay "Not Looking at Pictures." When the objective expert who accompanies the author through art galleries speaks of color, composition, and structural significance, he is voicing interpretations, though he would not call them that. Forster, however, is aware that interpretation guides vision. "Pictures are not easy to look at," he says. "They are intended to appeal to the eye, but, almost as if it were gazing at the sun itself, the eye often reacts by closing as soon as it catches sight of them. The mind takes charge and instead goes off on some alien vision. The mind has such a congenial time that it for-gets what set it going." Consequently, three very different painters—van Gogh, Corot, Michelangelo—induce the same mood "if the mind is undisciplined and uncontrolled by the eye," each painting the starting point for "the same course through dreamland or funland" and the viewer never experiencing any-thing new.

Forster's expert was alarmed that people should use an image of art as the point of departure for their own trains of thought. But what the expert fails to see is that there is another side to this process: while some evocative detail, "a tress of hair, the half-open door of a summerhouse, a Crivelli dessert, a Bosch fish-and-fiend salad," may rivet our attention and pull us away from what is there, our suspicions, our suppositions, our gentle or urgent inner promptings seek form and substance that, for us sighted ones, is derived from the visual world. As surely as the visual image can send us plunging into our inner pools, our need for substantiation compels us to surface again into the visual world, gasping for air. With new and hungry eyes, we seek what is before us, whether that be a swarm of mayflies or a van Gogh landscape. It is a cycle.

Spring brings one of the great anniversaries of my life, that time when one year ago I saw not the newlyweds, the photographer, the tree, the bridge, the river, the floodplains, or even myself as figure, but the mayfly. And at that moment of new vision, it was not the mayfly but I who ascended toward regions unseen, breaking the surface film, my many-lensed eyes shocked by a light suddenly direct and steady and hot instead of water-muted, rippling and cool. With wings still moist and crumpled, I moved through the swirling, unfigured field, hovering a moment on the cusp of certainty until my eyes pulled forth that one detail—the cloud hanging like smoke above land—that was my substantiation.

April 1990